# SEW ONE AND YOU'RE DONE

## Making a Quilt from a Single Block

### EVELYN SLOPPY

Martingale®
& COMPANY

Sew One and You're Done: Making a Quilt from a Single Block
© 2006 by Evelyn Sloppy

That Patchwork Place® is an imprint of Martingale & Company®.

Martingale & Company
20205 144th Avenue NE
Woodinville, WA 98072-8478 USA
www.martingale-pub.com

Printed in China
11 10 09 08 07 06   8 7 6 5 4 3 2 1

**Library of Congress Cataloging-in-Publication Data**
Library of Congress Control Number: 2006002329

ISBN-13: 978-1-56477-665-5
ISBN-10: 1-56477-665-4

## Mission Statement
Dedicated to providing quality products and service to inspire creativity.

## Credits
President: *Nancy J. Martin*
CEO: *Daniel J. Martin*
COO: *Tom Wierzbicki*
Publisher: *Jane Hamada*
Editorial Director: *Mary V. Green*
Managing Editor: *Tina Cook*
Technical Editor: *Cyndi Hershey*
Copy Editor: *Melissa Bryan*
Design Director: *Stan Green*
Illustrator: *Laurel Strand*
Text Designer: *Trina Craig*
Cover Designer: *Stan Green*
Photographer: *Brent Kane*

# DEDICATION

TO ALL THE quilters who make and donate quilts for hundreds of causes—the sick, the homeless, the abused, the injured. Giving back to our communities is healing to both the receiver and the giver.

I remember the day I walked into a meeting of the Lake Mayfield Quilters and saw the quilts they were making for cancer patients. The quilts were made of a single piece of fabric for the top, the batting, and the backing, simply tied and bound. The group needed to make 20 quilts a month and didn't have the time to make "real" quilt tops. I volunteered to piece quilt tops for them to finish. I went to my two quilt groups, Heartstring Quilters and Cowlitz Prairie Crazy Quilters, and enlisted their help in making quilt tops. Together, we now make enough quilts to donate to our local cancer-treatment center, with the excess going to another center and also to a military hospital in our area. A label is attached to each quilt that reads: "Believe in miracles, they happen every day. We're thinking of you. Lake Mayfield Quilters." The rewards are great. Not only are we helping others, but we also enjoy the days we spend together having potluck lunches, visiting, and making these quilts.

*Lake Mayfield Quilters tying pieced tops and sewing on bindings*

# CONTENTS

Introduction • 4

Let's Make Charity Quilts • 5

Quiltmaking Basics • 6

Easy Piecing Techniques • 10

Enlarging the Quilt • 11

Finishing the Quilt • 13

Quilts

    Best Friends • 18

    Cat Tails • 21

    Cranberry Fudge • 25

    Flannel Roses • 28

    Garden Magic • 31

    Porcelain Stars • 34

Pumpkins and Such • 37

Schooltime • 39

A Simple Basket • 42

Springtime • 46

Star Bright • 50

Star within a Star • 53

Stars and Stripes • 57

Starburst • 60

Strawberries 'n' Cream • 64

Triple Bear's Paw • 67

Vintage Star • 71

Wild Goose Chase • 74

Winter Dreams • 77

About the Author • 80

# INTRODUCTION

*Sew One and You're Done* began as a search for interesting new patterns for charity quilts. I wanted to make quilts that were quick and easy, yet visually appealing and fun to make. After trying several ideas, I settled on taking a traditional block, maybe changing it a bit, and then enlarging it to create a "big block." By working with a limited fabric palette, larger pieces of fabric, and only one large block, I could piece a quilt top in just a few hours, and the results were stunning. The quilts I made were lap sized, ranging from 45" to 56" square. I had such fun making these quilts that I just kept designing and piecing until I had completed the 19 quilts you'll find in this book. If you'd like to make these quilts for charity, I've included some tips on organizing group quilting sessions. These tips cover topics like getting the word out about your group; collecting fabrics, cutting, and sewing; and making the sessions fun for everybody involved.

Although I originally intended to make these quilts just for charity projects, I now find myself also making them as table toppers, wall hangings, and gifts. They're a great size for a baby quilt or as a lap quilt for a sick friend. They're so quick to sew, you could even make them for everybody on your Christmas list. They're easy enough for the beginning quilter, yet interesting enough for the more experienced quilter. I now like to keep a stash of these quilts on hand for gifts.

I've also shown how to enlarge the big blocks to make larger quilts by adding plain and pieced borders. Or, to make a queen- or king-size bed quilt, simply piece four blocks together. You'll also learn how to quickly finish your quilt, from tying or simple machine-quilting ideas to a fast machine-binding technique.

Now's a good time to pick a pattern and get started. And, for double the pleasure, how about making two quilts at the same time—one for you and one to give to a favorite charity.

*Heartstring Quilters with pieced tops they made for charity*

*Cowlitz Prairie Crazy Quilters with pieced tops to be made into donation quilts*

# LET'S MAKE CHARITY QUILTS

So you'd like to make charity quilts, but don't know how to get started? Here are a few tips I've learned along the way:

- Check with your local quilt shop or quilt guild. They usually have an organization to which they donate quilts, and would welcome your help. Often, they will have kits made up that you can take home and work on at your leisure.

- Organize a group of friends who would like to make these quilts, and find an organization that needs quilts. Check with hospitals, treatment centers, police departments, homeless centers, or social-service agencies. Also, don't forget organizations that don't need quilts but could use financial donations, such as your local animal shelter, fire department, or library. You could make the quilts and then sell, raffle, or auction them off and donate the proceeds.

- Decide on a time and place to meet. Someone's home is fine if the group is small, but if you need a larger space, check with your libraries, fire halls, or churches. Often, they will have space that they will be glad to let you use. Your local quilt shop may also have classroom space available.

- Ask everyone to bring what they can—fabric, batting, pearl cotton or crochet thread for tying, sewing machines and supplies, etc. Decide on the size of quilts you want to make and a few simple patterns to use.

- Organize the fabric, and start cutting and sewing. Let everybody do what they're comfortable doing. Some will enjoy cutting, while for others it will be ironing or sewing. Keep it simple and make sure everybody has a good time. You might prefer to just make up kits and let participants piece the quilt tops at home. Then you can finish the quilts at another group session.

- Once you've made some quilts, you'll need to promote your group. When your community knows what you're doing, you'll likely receive donations of fabric and cash. Generally, the only thing you'll have to buy is batting. Call your local newspaper to spread the word about your efforts; they might be interested in writing an article about your community service. Apply for financial grants to purchase supplies. Also, consider selling some of the quilts you make by raffle or auction. You can display the quilts in businesses around your community. Print a small brochure that tells about your group and what you're doing, and have copies of it available where you display a quilt. Your brochure should answer the following questions: What do we do? How did we start? When and where do we meet? How can you help? How can you reach us? The money from raffled or auctioned quilts can go toward buying batting or other supplies you might need. Check with your state first: you may need to register as a nonprofit organization if you plan to raffle or auction quilts.

- Make sure that your group has fun at your workshops. Potlucks are a great idea—we all work better on a full stomach. Welcome newcomers to your group by offering basic quilt-making lessons to anyone who wants to learn. Have drawings for prizes.

# QUILTMAKING BASICS

BEFORE GETTING STARTED, read this section to get an overview of quiltmaking, especially if you're a beginner. I include helpful information on choosing fabrics, rotary cutting, and accurate piecing.

## Fabric

SELECT HIGH-QUALITY, 100%-cotton fabrics. They hold their shape well and are easy to handle. Cotton flannels are also a good choice for these lap-sized quilts. Most of the quilts in this book have a limited fabric palette of two to five fabrics. I like to start out with a focus fabric. A focus fabric is a fabric I really love that is generally a multicolored print of medium to large scale. Then I choose fabrics that coordinate with the focus fabric, being sure to choose a range of light, medium, and dark fabrics. Keep in mind that the pieces for big-block quilts are larger than for most other quilts, so you can use larger prints that wouldn't work well in smaller blocks.

Make it a habit to wash and prepare fabrics after you purchase them. This ensures that your fabrics will be ready to sew when you are.

To begin, wash all fabrics first to preshrink, test for colorfastness, and get rid of excess dye. Continue to wash any dark fabrics until the rinse water is completely clear. Add a square of white fabric to each washing of the fabrics. When this white fabric remains its original color, the fabrics are colorfast.

After you wash and dry them, fold your fabrics neatly and store them. I don't press the fabrics yet, since I prefer to wait until I am ready to use them. When that time comes, I use spray sizing when pressing to restore body to the fabrics, since washing them removes the sizing. Spray sizing is especially helpful if you're working with bias edges, because the edges won't stretch out of shape as easily.

## Supplies

YOU'LL WANT TO keep the following tools and materials on hand.

**Rotary cutter and mat:** A large rotary cutter enables you to cut strips and pieces quickly without templates. A cutting mat is essential to protect both the blade and the table on which you're cutting. An 18" x 24" mat allows you to cut long strips, on the straight grain or across the bias. You might also consider purchasing a smaller mat to use when working with scraps.

**Rotary-cutting rulers:** Use a long, see-through ruler to measure and guide the rotary cutter. One that is 24" long is a good size. Try to find one that includes markings for 45° and 60° angles, guidelines for cutting strips, and standard measurements. Using such a specialized ruler improves cutting accuracy, makes quiltmaking more fun, and frees you from the frustrations that can result from inaccurate cuts.

**Sewing machine:** Stitching quilts on a sewing machine is easy and enjoyable. Spend some time getting to know your machine and becoming comfortable with its use. Keep your machine dust free and well oiled.

Machine piecing does not require an elaborate sewing machine. All you need is a straight-stitch machine in good working order. It should make an evenly locked straight stitch that looks the same on both sides of the fabric. Adjust the tension, if necessary, to produce smooth, even seams. A puckered seam can cause the fabric to curve, distorting the size and the shape of the pieced area as well as the entire quilt you're making.

**Pins:** Glass- or plastic-headed straight pins are excellent for pinning together patchwork pieces. Long pins are especially helpful when pinning thick layers together. If you plan to machine quilt, you'll need to hold the layers of the quilt together with a large supply of rustproof, size 2 safety pins.

**Needles:** Use sewing-machine needles sized for cotton fabrics (size 70/10 or 80/12). You also need hand-sewing needles (Sharps) and hand-quilting needles (Betweens, sizes 8, 9, or 10). For tying quilts, you'll need long darning or milliner's needles.

**Iron and ironing board:** Frequent and careful pressing is necessary to ensure a smooth, undistorted quilt top. Place your iron and ironing board, along with a plastic spray bottle of water, close to your sewing machine.

**Scissors:** Use good-quality shears, and use them only for cutting fabric. Thread snips or embroidery scissors are handy for clipping threads.

**Seam ripper:** This little tool will come in handy if you find it necessary to remove a seam before resewing.

**Thread:** For piecing, use a good-quality cotton or cotton-covered polyester thread.

## Rotary Cutting

Instructions for quick and easy rotary cutting are provided for each project. All measurements include standard ¼"-wide seam allowances. For those unfamiliar with rotary cutting, a brief introduction is provided in this section. For more-detailed information, see *The Quilter's Quick Reference Guide* by Candace Strick (Martingale & Company, 2004).

1. Fold the fabric and match the selvages, aligning the crosswise and lengthwise grains as much as possible. On the cutting mat, place the folded edge of the fabric closest to you. Align a square ruler, such as a Bias Square®, along the folded edge of the fabric. Place a long, straight ruler to the left of the square ruler, just covering the uneven raw edges along the left side of the fabric.

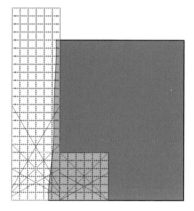

2. Remove the square ruler and cut along the right edge of the long ruler, rolling the rotary cutter away from you. Discard this strip. (Reverse this entire procedure if you're left-handed.)

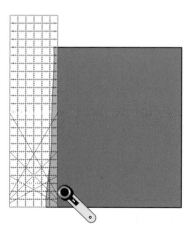

3. To cut strips, align the newly cut edge of the fabric with the appropriate ruler markings. For example, to cut a 3"-wide strip, place the 3" ruler marking at the edge of the fabric.

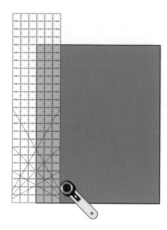

4. To cut squares, cut a strip of the required width. Trim the selvage ends and align the left edge of the strip with the desired ruler markings—the length measurement should equal the width measurement of the strip. Cut the strip into squares.

5. For rectangles, cut a strip the same width as the shorter side of the desired rectangle. Use the measurement of the longer side of the rectangle when cutting the strip into rectangles. For example, to cut a 3" x 5" rectangle, cut a 3"-wide strip and then cut 5"-long segments from it.

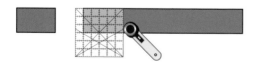

# Machine Piecing

Take the time to establish an exact ¼"-wide seam guide on your sewing machine. Some machines have a special quilting foot that measures exactly ¼" from the center needle position to the edge of the foot. This feature allows you to use the edge of the presser foot to guide the fabric for a perfect ¼"-wide seam allowance. If your machine doesn't have such a foot, create a seam guide by placing the edge of a piece of tape, moleskin, or a magnetic seam guide ¼" from the needle.

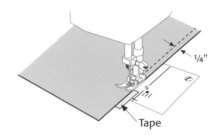

Do the following test to make sure you're sewing an accurate ¼"-wide seam.

1. Cut three strips of fabric, each 1½" x 3".

2. Sew the long edges of the strips together, using the edge of the presser foot or the seam guide you've made.

3. Press the seam allowances toward the outer edges.

4. Measure the center strip. After sewing and pressing, it should measure exactly 1" wide. If it doesn't, adjust the needle position or seam guide in the proper direction and repeat the test. I find that I need to sew with a scant ¼" seam (that is, about two threads less than ¼") in order for my measurements to come out correctly. This is because the pressing takes up a few threads. Try this if your sample strip is too small.

## Chain Piecing

Chain piecing is an efficient system that saves time and thread. The following steps describe the process.

1. Sew the first pair of pieces from cut edge to cut edge, using 12 stitches per inch. At the end of the seam, stop sewing but don't cut the thread.

2. Feed the next pair of pieces under the presser foot, as close as possible to the first pair. Continue feeding pieces through the machine without cutting the threads in between. There is no need to backstitch, since each seam will eventually be crossed and held by another seam.

3. When all the pieces have been sewn, remove the chain from the machine and clip the threads between the pieces.

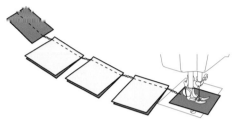

End sewing with
a thread saver.

## Easing

If two pieces being sewn together are slightly different in size (less than ⅛"), pin the places where the two pieces should match, and in between if necessary, to distribute the excess fabric evenly. With the longer piece on the bottom, sew the pieces together. The action of the feed dogs will help to ease the extra fabric into the seam.

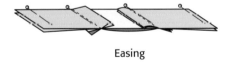

Easing

## Thread Savers

To save thread and prevent stray thread tails from shadowing through your quilt, use thread savers. Fold a 2" square of fabric in half (this is your first thread saver) and stitch across it from edge to edge; then with the presser foot down, feed pairs of quilt pieces through the machine as for chain piecing. When all the pieces are sewn together, sew across a second thread saver. Clip the threads between the pieces and reuse or discard the thread savers. This method eliminates trimming or having long threads hanging from your pieced blocks.

# Pressing

The traditional rule in quiltmaking is to press seam allowances to one side, toward the darker color wherever possible. First press the seam flat from the back of the fabric; then press the seam allowances in the desired direction from the front. Pressing is an up-and-down motion, as opposed to ironing, which is a back-and-forth motion used for removing wrinkles from clothes. To avoid distorting quilt pieces, be sure to press carefully by lifting and then lowering your iron onto the pieces without moving the iron from side to side. Press the seam allowances in the direction of the arrows in the project illustrations unless otherwise noted.

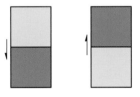

When joining two pieced units, plan ahead and press the seam allowances in opposite directions as shown. Pressing them in opposite directions reduces bulk and makes it easier to match seam lines. Where two seams meet, the seam allowances will butt against each other, making it easier to match seam intersections perfectly.

Opposing seams

# EASY PIECING TECHNIQUES

You'll see that my techniques for assembling big-block quilts differ from what I've used in my previous books. I've generally preferred to make my units slightly oversized and then trim them. However, in working with these oversized blocks, you're using fewer and larger pieces, and accuracy is more easily achieved. So, I save time by cutting the pieces the exact size I need, thus avoiding the trimming step. By carefully cutting your pieces and using accurate ¼" seam allowances, you'll be amazed at how quickly and accurately your block will come together.

## Bias Squares

Bias squares are units made of two contrasting half-square triangles sewn together on their long bias edges. They're usually made by cutting squares that are ⅞" larger than the desired finished size of the unit. The squares are then cut in half diagonally to yield two triangles, each with the straight grain on the two short sides.

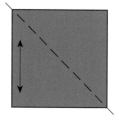
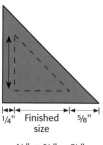

¼" Finished size ⅝"

¼" + ⅝" = ⅞"

## Quarter-Square-Triangle Units

Quarter-square-triangle units are pieced by sewing four triangles together on their bias edges. They're usually made by cutting squares that are 1¼" larger than the desired finished size of the unit. The squares are then cut diagonally in both directions to yield four triangles, each with the straight grain on the long side.

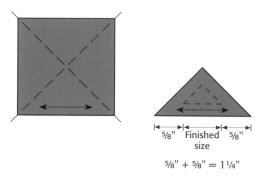

⅝" Finished size ⅝"

⅝" + ⅝" = 1¼"

## Combination Units

This unit combines a half-square triangle and two quarter-square triangles.

## Flying-Geese Units

The "geese" part of the unit (the larger triangle) is cut as a quarter-square triangle. The "sky" part of the unit (the two smaller triangles) is made by cutting half-square triangles.

# ENLARGING THE QUILT

After you've completed a big block, your quilt top is finished—no sewing together of blocks, sashing, and borders. One block is it. Following are some tips if you'd like a larger quilt that's lap sized or even bed sized.

**Simple borders:** The easiest way to make a quilt top bigger is to add a border or two. A single 5"- to 6"-wide border looks good; another option is a 2"- to 3"-wide inner border and a 5"- to 6"-wide outer border. If you'd like your quilt longer than it is wide, simply make the top and bottom borders wider than the side borders. You could also add corner squares to the borders for interest.

**Borders that echo the block design:** By adding a 5"- to 6"-wide border, followed by a pieced border mirroring the elements in your center block, followed by another 5"- to 6"-wide border, you could increase the size of your quilt from 48" to 84" square, adequate for a double or queen bed.

Simple border

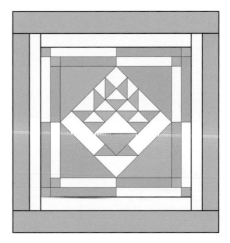

Two simple borders

Plain and pieced borders

Two borders with corner squares

**Multiple blocks:** Make four big blocks for a king-size quilt, 96" to 100" square, as shown below.

**Enlarging the big-block grid:** Note that most of the blocks used in these quilts are drafted in either an 8 x 8 grid or a 10 x 10 grid. By increasing the size of the grid, you can enlarge the quilt. For example, if each of the divisions in a 10 x 10 grid is 5", the quilt will be 50" square. By increasing the size to 10", you can enlarge the quilt to 100" square. Refer to "Easy Piecing Techniques" on page 10 to determine the size of the pieces you'll need to cut. For instance, to make a 5" finished bias square, you'll cut squares that are 5⅞". To increase this to a 10" finished bias square, you'll cut squares that are 10⅞". In the same manner, you could also reduce the size of the quilt to make a smaller wall hanging.

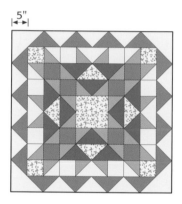

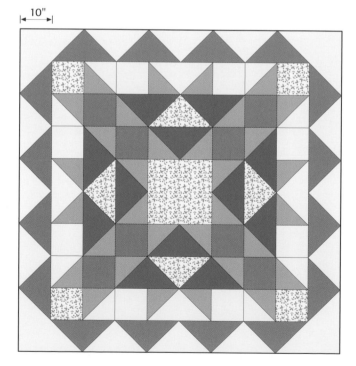

# FINISHING THE QUILT

The words "sew one and you're done" don't tell the full story. You still have to finish the quilt, which includes piecing the backing, layering and basting the layers, tying or quilting the layers to secure them, and then applying the binding. The following instructions will help you through this process, and then you really are done.

## Backing

If you use 42"-wide fabric for your quilt backing, all the projects in this book will require you to piece the backing from two widths of fabric. To do this, first remove the selvages along both long edges of the backing-fabric pieces. Join the pieces with a ½" seam and press the seam open.

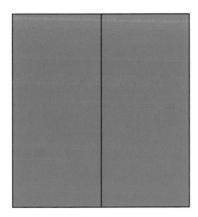

Two-piece backing

Since none of the quilts is *much* wider than a 42" width of fabric, you can reduce the amount of backing fabric you need to buy by simply sewing a wide border to both sides of one width of fabric. You could piece together scraps of fabric from your stash to make these borders. However, this is most effective when you use some of the fabrics that were used on the front of the quilt. If you decide to make a pieced backing in this manner, you'll need only half of the fabric yardage indicated.

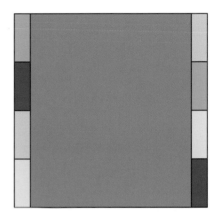

Backing with side borders

## Layering and Basting

Batting is available in several weights or layers. Thick battings are fine for tied quilts; a thinner batting is better, however, if you intend to quilt by hand or machine. Choose your batting and piece the backing fabric as needed. The materials list with each project allows enough yardage for the backing fabric to create a 4" margin around all sides of the quilt top, if desired. The batting sizes allow for 2" on all sides. Since the idea behind *Sew One and You're Done* is to make the process quick and easy, you'll probably decide to tie or machine quilt. If you do want to hand quilt using any decorative designs, you should mark the quilting design on your quilt top before you layer it with batting and backing.

To layer your quilt, place the backing on a table with the wrong side of the fabric facing up. Secure the backing with masking tape to keep it taut and smooth. Spread your batting over the backing, centering it and smoothing out any folds or wrinkles. Center the pressed quilt top on these two layers, right side up. Check that there is adequate batting and backing on all sides. If the quilt is larger than the tabletop, let the excess hang down the sides of the table, baste the part of the quilt that's on the table, and then move the quilt up and baste the remaining area.

Once your quilt is layered, it is ready for tying or (if you plan to quilt by hand or machine) basting. The basting method you use depends on whether you'll quilt by hand or by machine. Thread basting is generally used for hand quilting, whereas safety-pin basting is used for machine quilting. Space the stitching lines or pins about 4" apart.

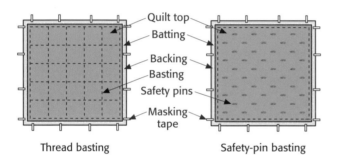

Thread basting          Safety-pin basting

## Tying

Tying your quilt is the fastest way to finish it, so it is popular for charity quilts. Tying also allows you to use one of the thicker poly battings, which makes for a very fluffy quilt and is quite nice for baby quilts. I like to use #8 pearl cotton, but crochet threads work well, too. For best results, place your ties no more than 6" apart. Evenly space the ties, trying to place them at all major intersections.

Thread a large or darning needle with an approximate 60" length of thread, but don't knot the end. Choose a place along an edge of the quilt where you'd like to make a tie. Insert the needle down through all the layers and come up approximately 1/8" away. Move to the next spot to be tied, insert the needle, and take a small stitch. Don't cut the thread. Continue across the quilt in one direction until

you've run out of thread. Clip the threads about halfway between the stitches. Tie a square knot at each point, and trim off any excess thread if the tails are too long. Start again with another 60" length of thread, and repeat until you've completed the quilt.

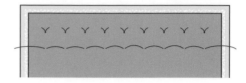

## Machine Quilting

A walking foot or even-feed foot is essential for straight-line quilting and for large, simple curves. The foot helps feed the quilt layers through the machine without shifting or puckering. Read your machine's instruction manual for help with special tension settings to sew through extra fabric layers.

Use a darning foot and lower the feed dogs for free-motion quilting. Free-motion quilting allows the fabric to move freely under the foot of the sewing machine. Because the feed dogs are lowered, the stitch length is determined by the speed at which you run the machine and feed the fabric under the darning foot. Practice on layers of fabric scraps until you get the feel of controlling the motion of the fabric with your hands. Run the machine fairly fast, since this makes it easier to sew smoother lines of quilting. Don't turn the fabric under the needle. Instead, guide the fabric as if it were under a stationary pencil (the needle).

Stitch some free-form scribbles, zigzags, and curves. Try a heart or a star. Free-motion quilting may feel awkward at first, but with a little determination and practice, you can imitate beautiful hand-quilting designs quickly and complete a project in just a few hours.

# Binding

You can cut strips across the width of fabric or on the bias of the fabric to make a French double-fold binding that rolls over edges nicely and has two layers of fabric to resist wear. You'll need enough strips to go around the perimeter of the quilt, plus 10" for seams and the corners in a mitered fold.

To make strips for bias binding, open your binding fabric and lay it flat in a single layer. Align the 45° line on your rotary-cutting ruler with one of the selvage edges of the fabric. Cut along the ruler edge and trim off the corner. Cut 2½"-wide strips, measuring from the edge of the initial bias cut. Note that for quilts with rounded corners, bias binding is necessary as it provides the "give" required to stretch around the outside curves.

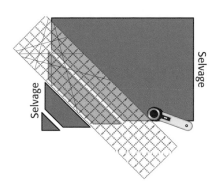

Once you cut the strips for binding (bias or straight grain), follow these steps to join the strips and attach the binding:

1. With right sides together, join the strips at right angles and stitch on the diagonal as shown. Trim the excess fabric and press the seam allowances open to make one long piece of binding.

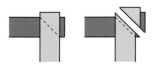
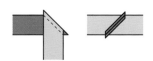

Joining straight-cut strips    Joining bias strips

2. Fold the strip in half lengthwise, wrong sides together, and press.

3. Trim the batting and backing so that it extends ¼" beyond the quilt top. This extra material will fill up the binding when you attach it so that the binding isn't flat.

4. Use a walking foot, if you have one, for attaching the binding. The foot is helpful in feeding all the layers of the quilt evenly through the machine. Starting near the middle of one side, align the raw edges of the binding with the quilt top. Leaving the first 10" or so of the binding free, stitch the binding to the quilt toward the first corner. End the stitching ¼" from the corner of the quilt and backstitch. Clip the thread.

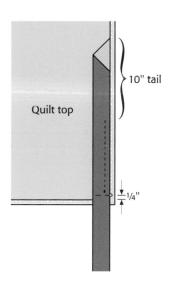

5. Turn the quilt so that you'll be stitching down the next side. Fold the binding up, away from the quilt, with the raw edges aligned.

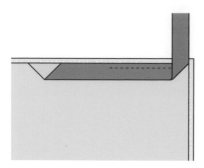

6. Fold the binding back down onto itself, even with the edge of the quilt top. Begin stitching at the corner.

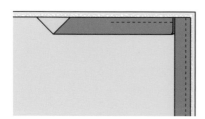

7. Repeat the process on the remaining edges and corners of the quilt. Stop sewing about 15" from where you began. Lay the beginning of the binding flat on the quilt top. Overlap the end of the binding over the beginning. Trim the end so that the overlap measures 2½". (This overlap should be equal to the width of your binding strip.)

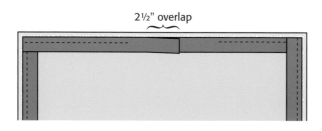

2½" overlap

8. Open up the beginning and ending of the binding and place them right sides together at a right angle as shown. Draw a diagonal line and secure the binding with pins.

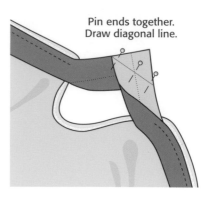

Pin ends together.
Draw diagonal line.

9. Stitch on the diagonal line. Check to make sure you've stitched correctly before trimming the seam allowance to ¼". Press the seam allowance open.

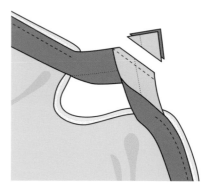

10. Refold the binding in half, laying it flat along the quilt edge. Then finish sewing the binding to the top.

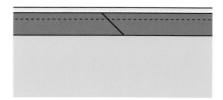

11. Fold the binding over the raw edges of the quilt to the back of the quilt, with the folded edge covering the row of machine stitching. Blindstitch the binding in place. A miter will form at each corner. Blindstitch the mitered corners in place.

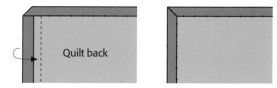

## Rounded Corners

I love to make rounded corners on my quilts. It's so much easier because you don't have to miter the corners of the binding. After the quilt is quilted, use a dinner plate as a guide to mark and trim the corners. Be sure to center the plate evenly over each corner. For a project with rounded corners, you'll want to make bias binding so that it will ease around the corners nicely.

## Quick Machine Binding

I prefer the look of traditional binding, in which the binding is folded over the raw edges of the quilt to the back and then stitched down by hand. However, sometimes I need to use a quicker method. This method is ideal for charity quilts.

Make the binding as shown above, but attach it to the back of the quilt, instead of to the front. Place the raw edges of the binding about ¼" from the back edge of the quilt as you stitch. After the binding is attached, fold the binding over the raw edges of the quilt to the front, with the folded edge covering the row of machine stitching. Stitch the binding in place, using either a straight, zigzag, or decorative stitch.

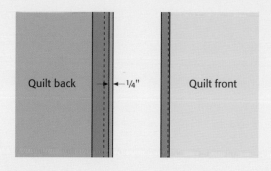

# Best Friends

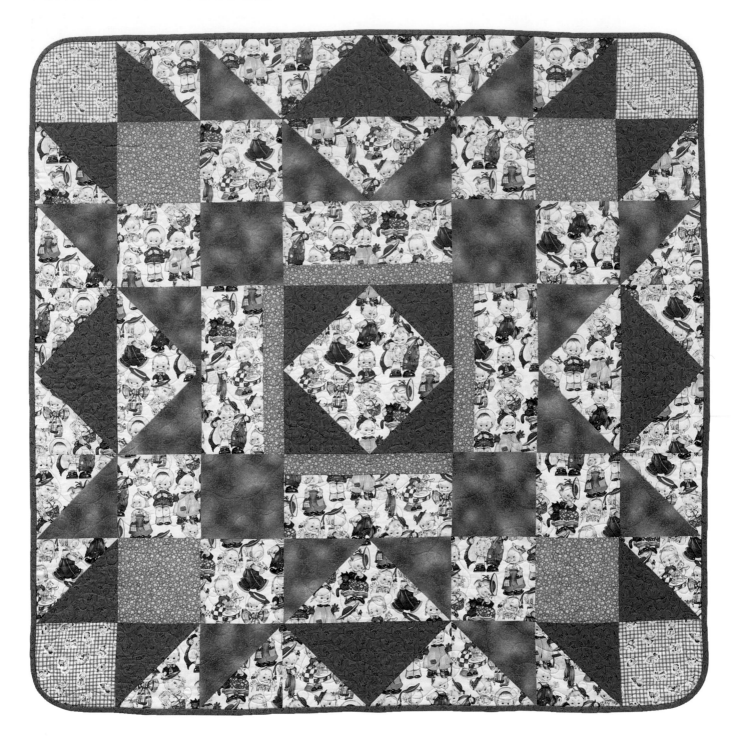

*48" x 48"; by Evelyn Sloppy, 2005*

# Materials

*All yardages are based on 42"-wide fabric.*

1¾ yards of theme print for piecing★

1⅛ yards of blue print for piecing (¾ yard) and binding (⅝ yard)

⅔ yard of orange print for piecing

⅜ yard of green print 1 for piecing★★

¼ yard of green print 2 for piecing★★

3¼ yards of fabric for backing

52" x 52" piece of batting

★ *You'll need 2 yards if you're using a directional print.*

★★ *You could use ⅝ yard of just one green fabric.*

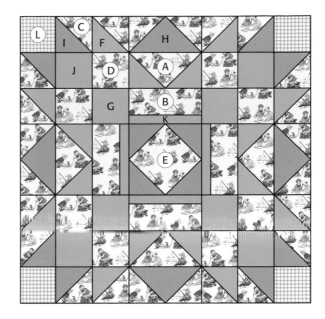

# Cutting

| Fabric | Piece | Strips | Width | First Cut | Second Cut |
|---|---|---|---|---|---|
| Theme print★ | A | 1 | 13¼" | 1 square, 13¼" x 13¼" | ⊠ |
| | B | From remainder of A strip | | 4 rectangles, 5" x 12½" | |
| | C | 3 | 6⅞" | 12 squares, 6⅞" x 6⅞" | ◹ |
| | D | 2 | 6½" | 8 squares, 6½" x 6½" | |
| | E | 1 | 9" | 1 square, 9" x 9" | |
| Orange print | F | 2 | 6⅞" | 8 squares, 6⅞" x 6⅞" | ◹ |
| | G | 1 | 6½" | 4 squares, 6½" x 6½" | |
| Blue print | H | 1 | 13¼" | 1 square, 13¼" x 13¼" | ⊠ |
| | I | From remainder of H strip | | 1 square, 6⅞" x 6⅞" | ◹ |
| | I | 1 | 6⅞" | 5 squares, 6⅞" x 6⅞" | ◹ |
| | Binding | 6 | 2½" | | |
| Green print 1 | J | 1 | 6½" | 4 squares, 6½" x 6½" | |
| | K | 2 | 2" | 4 rectangles, 2" x 12½" | |
| Green print 2 | L | 1 | 6½" | 4 squares, 6½" x 6½" | |

★ If you're using a directional print, cut as follows:

- Cut the B rectangles so that 2 have the long sides perpendicular to the selvages (crosswise grain) and 2 have the long sides parallel to the selvages (lengthwise grain). This way, the figures on the fabric will all be upright on your quilt.
- Cut the C squares so that half are cut diagonally from upper left to lower right, and the other half diagonally from lower left to upper right. 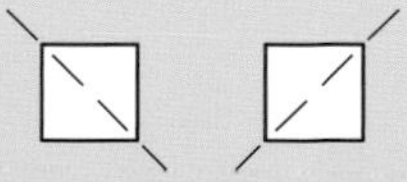
- Cut the E square on point so that the figures on the fabric will be upright on your quilt. You may want to first make a template for this shape and then trace it and cut the fabric.

It does take a little extra care to use directional prints, but they're well worth the effort. Cut and lay out all the pieces before you start sewing, making sure that the directional prints are facing upright. By carefully cutting your pieces as directed, each one will be in an upright position somewhere in the quilt.

## Piecing

After stitching each unit, press seam allowances as indicated by arrows in the illustrations.

1. For the center section, sew a blue I triangle to each side of the theme-print E square.

2. Sew a theme-print B rectangle to a green K rectangle, joining their long sides. Repeat to make four units.

Make 4.

3. Sew a theme-print C triangle to an orange F triangle to make a bias square. Repeat to make eight units. In the same manner, sew a theme-print C triangle to a blue I triangle. Repeat to make eight units.

Make 8.        Make 8.

4. Sew an orange F triangle to each end of a theme-print A triangle to make a flying-geese unit. Repeat to make four units. In the same manner, make four flying-geese units using the remaining theme-print C triangles and blue H triangles.

Make 4.        Make 4.

5. Arrange and sew two theme-print D squares, one orange G square, one green print J square, one green print L square, and four of the bias squares made in step 3 into rows. Sew the rows together. Repeat to make four corner units.

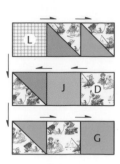

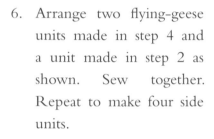

Make 4.

6. Arrange two flying-geese units made in step 4 and a unit made in step 2 as shown. Sew together. Repeat to make four side units.

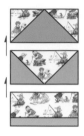

Make 4.

7. Arrange and sew the center section, corner units, and side units into rows. Sew the rows together.

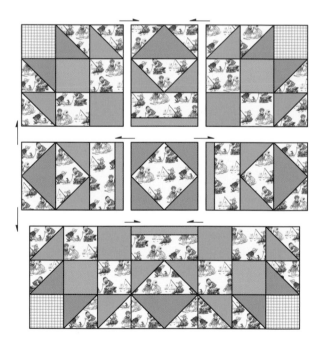

## Finishing

Referring to "Finishing the Quilt" on page 13, piece the backing and then layer the quilt top with the batting and backing. After basting the layers together, quilt or tie as desired. Refer to "Rounded Corners" on page 17 to shape and bind the edges of the quilt.

# Cat Tails

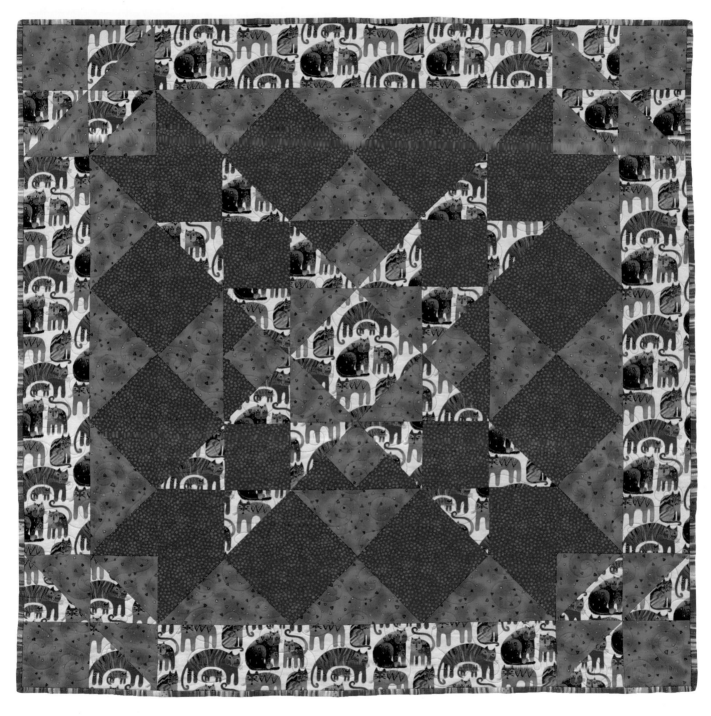

*50″ x 50″; by Evelyn Sloppy, 2005*

# Materials

1⅜ yards of blue print for piecing

1⅓ yards of theme print for piecing★

1½ yards of orange print for piecing

3⅜ yards of fabric for backing

½ yard of binding fabric

54" x 54" piece of batting

★ *Yardage is sufficient for directional prints.*

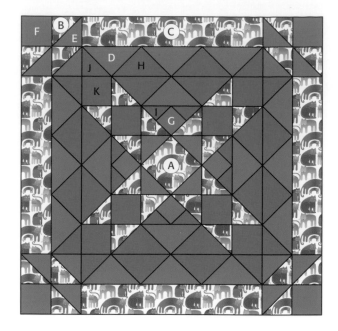

# Cutting

| Fabric | Piece | Strips | Width | First Cut | Second Cut |
|---|---|---|---|---|---|
| Theme print★ | A | 1 | 7½" | 1 square, 7½" x 7½" | |
| | B | From remainder of A strip | | 2 squares, 5⅞" x 5⅞" | ◹ |
| | B | 2 | 5⅞" | 12 squares, 5⅞" x 5⅞" | ◹ |
| | C | 4 | 5½" | 4 rectangles, 5½" x 30½" | |
| Blue print | D | 2 | 11¼" | 4 squares, 11¼" x 11¼" | ⊠ |
| | E | 2 | 5⅞" | 8 squares, 5⅞" x 5⅞" | ◹ |
| | F | 1 | 5½" | 4 squares, 5½" x 5½" | |
| | G | 1 | 4" | 4 squares, 4" x 4" | |
| Orange print | H | 2 | 11¼" | 4 squares, 11¼" x 11¼" | ⊠ |
| | I | 1 | 6¼" | 2 squares, 6¼" x 6¼" | ⊠ |
| | J | 1 | 5⅞" | 4 squares, 5⅞" x 5⅞" | ◹ |
| | K | 2 | 5½" | 8 squares, 5½" x 5½" | |
| Binding | | 6 | 2½" | | |

★ If you're using a directional print, as in the quilt shown, cut as follows:

- Cut 2 strips, 5½" wide; crosscut into 2 C rectangles, 5½" x 30½".
- Cut 2 C rectangles, 5½" x 30½", on the lengthwise grain of the fabric, so that the figures on the fabric will all be upright on your quilt.
- From the remaining fabric, cut 4 strips, 5⅞" wide; crosscut into 14 B squares, 5⅞" x 5⅞". Cut half of these squares diagonally from upper left to lower right, and the other half diagonally from lower left to upper right. 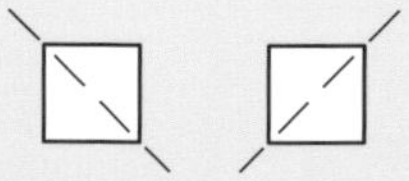
- Cut the A square on point so that the figures on the fabric will be upright on your quilt. You may want to first make a template for this shape and then trace it and cut the fabric.

It does take a little extra care to use directional prints, but they're well worth the effort. You should cut and lay out all the pieces before you start sewing, making sure that the directional prints are facing upright. By carefully cutting your pieces as directed, each one will be in an upright position somewhere in the quilt.

# Piecing

The many triangles in this quilt form quite a few multipoint intersections. I like to press all the seams open to reduce the bulk. Give it a try; you might also prefer this method. However, arrows have been provided in the illustrations to indicate traditional pressing methods.

1. Sew a blue E triangle to each side of the theme-print A square.

Make 1.

2. Sew an orange I triangle to adjacent sides of a blue G square. Sew theme-print B triangles to the short sides of the unit. Repeat to make four units.

Make 4.

3. Sew units made in step 2 to opposite sides of the unit made in step 1. Sew an orange K square to each end of the two remaining units made in step 2. Sew these units to the top and bottom of the center to complete the center star.

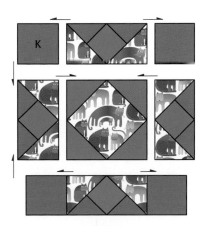

Make 1.

4. Sew together one blue D triangle, two orange H triangles, and two theme-print B triangles as shown. Repeat to make four units.

Make 4

5. Sew units made in step 4 to opposite sides of the center star. Sew orange K squares to each end of the two remaining units made in step 4. Sew these units to the top and bottom of the center star.

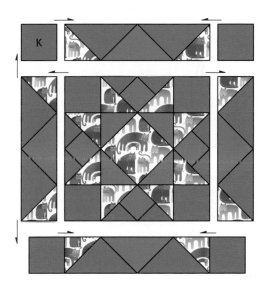

Make 1.

6. Sew together three blue D triangles, two orange H triangles, and two orange J triangles as shown. Sew a theme-print C rectangle to the unit along the blue-triangle edge. Repeat to make four units.

Make 4.

7. Sew a theme-print B triangle to a blue E triangle to make a bias square. Repeat to make 12 bias squares. Sew together three bias squares and a blue F square as shown. Repeat to make four corner units.

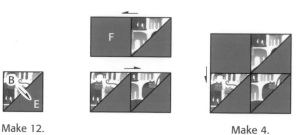

Make 12.                                          Make 4.

8. Sew units made in step 6 to opposite sides of the center star as shown. Sew a corner unit made in step 7 to each end of the two remaining units made in step 6. Sew these to the top and bottom of the center star to complete the quilt.

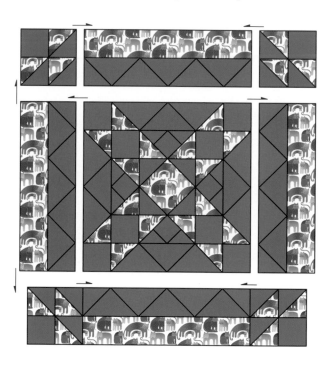

# Finishing

Referring to "Finishing the Quilt" on page 13, piece the backing and then layer the quilt top with the batting and backing. After basting the layers together, quilt or tie as desired. Prepare the binding and sew it to the quilt.

## Quilting Suggestion

To complement the cats in my theme print, I quilted this project with a stipple design that resembles curling cats' tails.

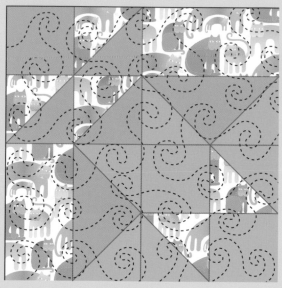

Cat tails stipple

# Cranberry Fudge

*48" x 48"; by Evelyn Sloppy, 2005*

# Materials

*All yardages are based on 42"-wide fabric.*

1⅛ yards of cranberry print for piecing (⅝ yard) and binding (½ yard)

⅞ yard of dark brown print for piecing

¾ yard of light brown print for piecing

⅝ yard of medium brown print for piecing

3¼ yards of fabric for backing

52" x 52" piece of batting

# Cutting

| Fabric | Piece | Strips | Width | Cut |
|---|---|---|---|---|
| Dark brown print | A | 1 | 8½" | 4 squares, 8½" x 8½" |
| | B | 3 | 4½" | Cut 2 strips only into 8 rectangles, 4½" x 8½" |
| | C | 1 | 4½" | |
| Light brown print | D | 1 | 8½" | 1 square, 8½" x 8½" |
| | F | From remainder of D strip | | 4 squares, 4½" x 4½" |
| | E | 1 | 4½" | |
| | F | 2 | 4½" | |
| Cranberry print | G | 3 | 4½" | 12 rectangles, 4½" x 8½" |
| | H | 1 | 4½" | |
| | Binding | 6 | 2½" | |
| Medium brown print | I | 2 | 8½" | 8 squares, 8½" x 8½" |

# Piecing

After stitching each unit, press seam allowances as indicated by arrows in the illustrations.

1. Sew a light brown E strip and a dark brown B strip together along their long sides. Crosscut into four 8½" segments.

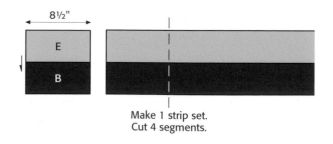

Make 1 strip set.
Cut 4 segments.

2. Sew a light brown F strip and a cranberry H strip together along their long sides. Crosscut into eight 4½" segments. In the same manner, sew a light brown F strip and a dark brown C strip together. Crosscut into eight 4½" segments.

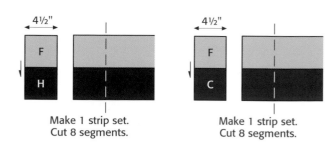

Make 1 strip set.
Cut 8 segments.

Make 1 strip set.
Cut 8 segments.

3. Sew a cranberry G rectangle to a cranberry/light brown segment made in step 2. Repeat to make four units.

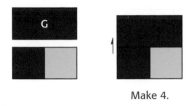

Make 4.

4. Sew units made in step 1 to opposite sides of a light brown D square as shown. Sew units made in step 3 to each end of the remaining units made in step 1. Sew these to the top and bottom to make the center unit.

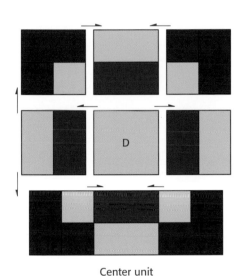

Center unit

5. Sew medium brown I squares to opposite sides of a dark brown A square. Sew a dark brown B rectangle to each end of a cranberry G rectangle. Repeat to make four of each unit. Sew one of each unit together. Repeat to make four units.

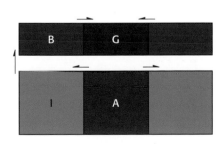

Make 4.

6. Sew together two dark brown/light brown units and one cranberry/light brown unit made in step 2. Repeat to make four units. Sew a light brown F square to a cranberry G rectangle. Sew this to the six-patch unit. Repeat to make four units.

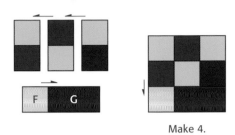

Make 4.

7. Sew units made in step 5 to opposite sides of the center unit. Sew a unit made in step 6 to each end of the remaining units as shown. Sew these to the top and bottom of the center unit to complete the quilt.

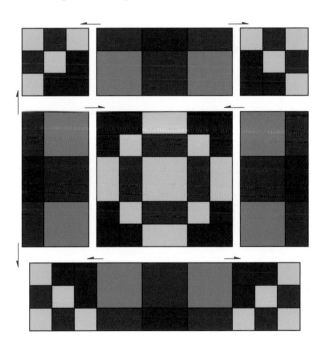

# Finishing

Referring to "Finishing the Quilt" on page 13, piece the backing and then layer the quilt top with the batting and backing. After basting the layers together, quilt or tie as desired. Refer to "Rounded Corners" on page 17 to shape and bind the edges of the quilt.

# Flannel Roses

*48″ x 48″; by Evelyn Sloppy, 2005*

## Materials

*All yardages are based on 42″-wide fabric.*

1 yard of red print 1 for piecing and binding (½ yard for piecing and ½ yard for binding)

⅓ yard of red print 2 for piecing (If using a stripe, you'll need ⅝ yard.)

⅓ yard of red print 3 for piecing

⅝ yard of brown print 1 for piecing

⅓ yard of brown print 2 for piecing

⅝ yard of light brown print for piecing

⅓ yard of red-and-white print 1 for piecing

⅓ yard of red-and-white print 2 for piecing

⅓ yard of red-and-white print 3 for piecing

3¼ yards of fabric for backing

52" x 52" piece of batting

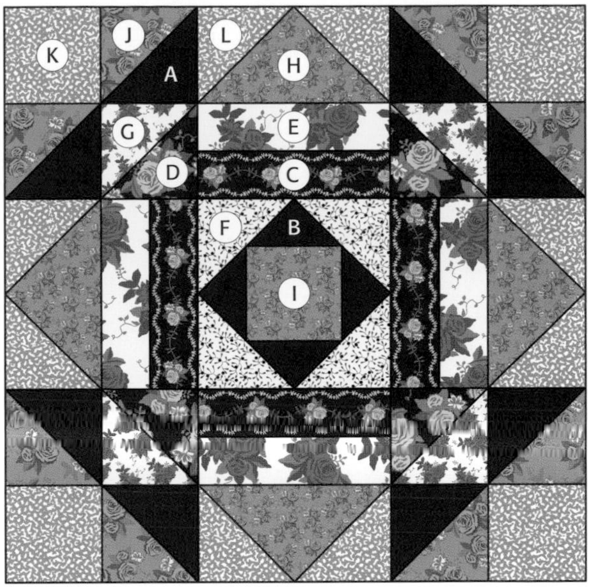


**Note:** *I didn't have enough of any single red, red-and-white, or brown print to make this quilt, so I just combined two or three prints of each and they work beautifully together. If you want to use just one print of each, you'll need:*

- *1⅝ yards of red print*
- *⅝ yard of red-and-white print*
- *⅞ yard of brown print*

## Cutting

| Fabric | Piece | Strips | Width | First Cut | Second Cut |
|---|---|---|---|---|---|
| Red print 1 | A | 1 | 8⅞" | 4 squares, 8⅞" x 8⅞" (A) | ⧅ |
| | B | 1 | 6¼" | 2 squares, 6¼" x 6¼" (B) | ⧅ |
| | Binding | 6 | 2½" | | |
| Red print 2* | C | 2 | 4½" | 4 rectangles, 4½" x 16½" | |
| Red print 3 | D | 1 | 8⅞" | 2 squares, 8⅞" x 8⅞" | ⧅ |
| Red-and-white print 1 | E | 2 | 4½" | 4 rectangles, 4½" x 16½" | |
| Red-and-white print 2 | F | 1 | 8⅞" | 2 squares, 8⅞" x 8⅞" | ⧅ |
| Red-and-white print 3 | G | 1 | 8⅞" | 2 squares, 8⅞" x 8⅞" | ⧅ |
| Brown print 1 | H | 1 | 17¼" | 1 square, 17¼" x 17¼" | ⊠ |
| | I | From remainder of H strip | | 1 square, 8½" x 8½" | |
| Brown print 2 | J | 1 | 8⅞" | 4 squares, 8⅞" x 8⅞" | ⧅ |
| Light brown print | K | 1 | 8½" | 4 squares, 8½" x 8½" | |
| | L | 1 | 8⅞" | 4 squares, 8⅞" x 8⅞" | ⧅ |

* If using a stripe, cut the 4 C rectangles with the long sides parallel to the selvage (lengthwise grain). Center the stripe motifs within each rectangle.

# Piecing

After stitching each unit, press seam allowances as indicated by arrows in the illustrations.

1. Sew the four red B triangles to opposite sides of the brown I square. In the same manner, add the four red-and-white F triangles to complete the center unit.

 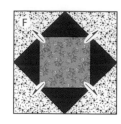

Center unit

2. Sew a red-and-white G triangle to a red D triangle to make a bias square. Repeat to make four units. In the same manner, sew a brown J triangle to a red A triangle. Repeat to make eight units.

Make 4.  Make 8.

3. Sew a red-and-white E rectangle to a red C rectangle. Repeat to make four units.

Make 4.

4. Sew units made in step 3 to opposite sides of the center unit as shown. Sew the red/red-and-white bias squares made in step 2 to each end of the remaining units made in step 3. Sew these units to the top and bottom of the center unit.

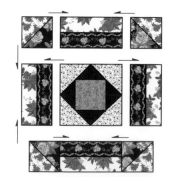

5. Sew light brown L triangles to the short sides of a brown H triangle to make a flying-geese unit. Repeat to make four units. Sew a brown/red bias square made in step 2 to each end of the flying-geese units.

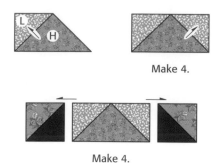

Make 4.

Make 4.

6. Sew units made in step 5 to opposite sides of the center unit. Sew a light brown K square to each end of the remaining units made in step 5. Sew these units to the top and bottom of the center unit to complete the quilt top.

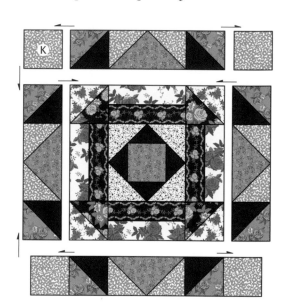

# Finishing

Referring to "Finishing the Quilt" on page 13, piece the backing and then layer the quilt top with the batting and backing. After basting the layers together, quilt or tie as desired. Prepare the binding and sew it to the quilt.

# Garden Magic

*48" x 48"; by Evelyn Sloppy, 2005*

# Materials

*All yardages are based on 42"-wide fabric.*

1⅓ yards of blue print for piecing (⅞ yard) and
binding (½ yard)

1⅛ yards of green print for piecing

1 yard of light print for piecing

3¼ yards of fabric for backing

52" x 52" piece of batting

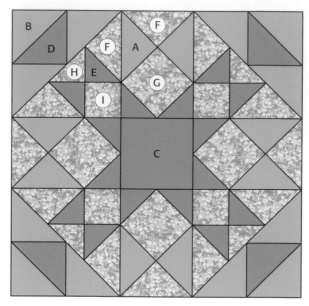

# Cutting

| Fabric | Piece | Strips | Width | First Cut | Second Cut |
|---|---|---|---|---|---|
| Green print | A | 1 | 13¼" | 2 squares, 13¼" x 13¼" | ⊠ |
|  | B | 2 | 9⅞" | 6 squares, 9⅞" x 9⅞" | ◺ |
| Blue print | C | 1 | 12½" | 1 square, 12½" x 12½" |  |
|  | D | From remainder of C strip |  | 2 squares, 9⅞" x 9⅞" | ◺ |
|  | E | 2 | 6⅞" | 8 squares, 6⅞" x 6⅞" | ◺ |
|  | Binding | 6 | 2½" |  |  |
| Light print | F | 1 | 13¼" | 3 squares, 13¼" x 13¼" | ⊠ |
|  | G | 1 | 9" | 4 squares, 9" x 9" |  |
|  | H | 1 | 6⅞" | 2 squares, 6⅞" x 6⅞" | ◺ |
|  | I | From remainder of H strip |  | 4 squares, 6½" x 6½" |  |

# Piecing

After stitching each unit, press seam allowances as
indicated by arrows in the illustrations.

1. Sew a green B triangle to a blue D triangle to
   make a bias square. Sew green B triangles to the
   blue sides of the bias square. Repeat to make
   four units.

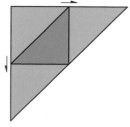

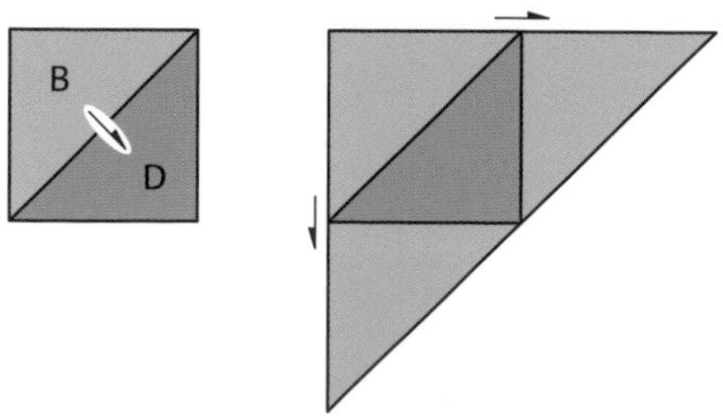

Make 4.

2. Sew a light H triangle to the short side of a blue
   E triangle as shown. Sew a light F triangle to
   the long side of the blue E triangle. Make four
   units.

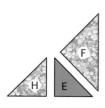

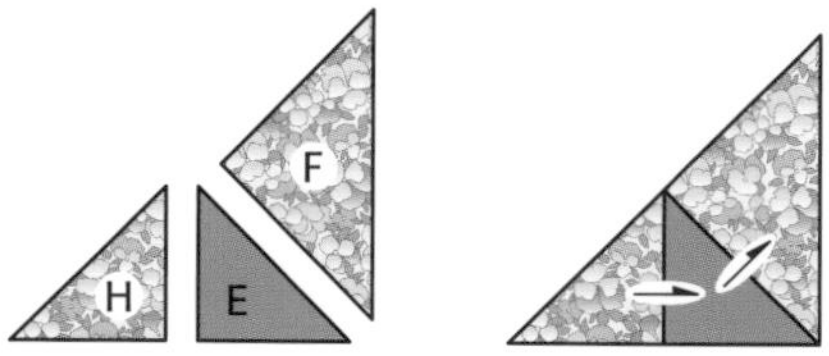

Make 4.

3. Sew a blue E triangle to the short side of a light F triangle as shown. Sew a light I square to the blue E triangle as shown. Make four units.

Make 4.

4. Sew a unit made in step 2 to a unit made in step 3 as shown. Make four units.

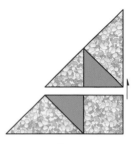

Make 4.

5. Sew a unit made in step 1 to a unit made in step 4. Repeat to make four units.

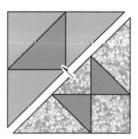

Make 4.

6. Sew a green A triangle to a light F triangle as shown. Make four units.

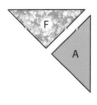 

Make 4.

7. Sew a green A triangle to a light G square. Sew a blue E triangle to the opposite side of the light

G square. Sew another blue E triangle to the light G square as shown. Make four units.

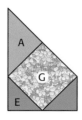 

Make 4.

8. Sew a unit made in step 6 to a unit made in step 7. Make four units.

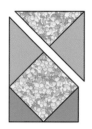 

Make 4.

9. Arrange and sew the four units made in step 5, the four units made in step 8, and the blue C square into rows. Sew the rows together.

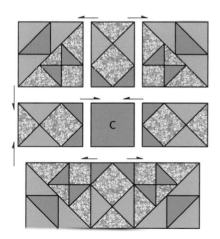

## Finishing

Referring to "Finishing the Quilt" on page 13, piece the backing and then layer the quilt top with the batting and backing. After basting the layers together, quilt or tie as desired. Prepare the binding and sew it to the quilt.

# Porcelain Stars

*48" x 48"; by Evelyn Sloppy, 2005*

# Materials

*All yardages are based on 42″-wide fabric.*

1½ yards of dark blue print for piecing (1 yard)
   and binding (½ yard)

1⅓ yards of light blue print for piecing

⅞ yard of medium blue print for piecing

3¼ yards of fabric for backing

52" x 52" piece of batting

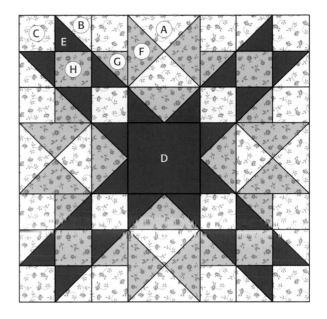

# Cutting

| Fabric | Piece | Strips | Width | First Cut | Second Cut |
|--------|-------|--------|-------|-----------|------------|
| Light blue | A | 1 | 13¼" | 2 squares, 13¼" x 13¼" | ⊠ |
| | B | 1 | 6⅞" | 4 squares, 6⅞" x 6⅞" | ◩ |
| | C | 3 | 6½" | 16 squares, 6½" x 6½" | |
| Dark blue | D | 1 | 12½" | 1 square, 12½" x 12½" | |
| | E | 3 | 6⅞" | 12 squares, 6⅞" x 6⅞" | ◩ |
| | Binding | 6 | 2½" | | |
| Medium blue | F | 1 | 13¼" | 3 squares, 13¼" x 13¼" | ⊠ |
| | G | 1 | 6⅞" | 4 squares, 6⅞" x 6⅞" | ◩ |
| | H | 1 | 6½" | 4 squares, 6½" x 6½" | |

# Piecing

After stitching each unit, press seam allowances as indicated by arrows in the illustrations.

1. Sew a dark blue E triangle to each short side of a medium blue F triangle to make a flying-geese unit. Repeat to make four units.

  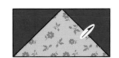

Make 4.

2. Sew a light blue A triangle to a medium blue F triangle as shown. Repeat to make eight units. Sew these units together in pairs to make four quarter-square-triangle units.

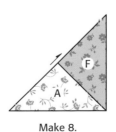  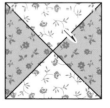

Make 8.          Make 4.

3. Sew a quarter-square-triangle unit made in step 2 to a flying-geese unit made in step 1 as shown. Repeat to make four units.

Make 4.

4. Sew a light blue B triangle to a dark blue E triangle to make a bias square. In the same manner, sew a medium blue G triangle to a dark blue E triangle. Repeat to make eight of each unit.

Make 8.　　Make 8.

5. Arrange and sew four light blue C squares, one medium blue H square, and two bias squares of each color combination into rows. Sew the rows together to make a corner unit. Repeat to make four units.

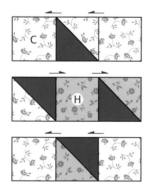 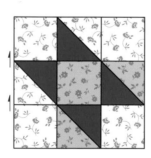

Make 4.

6. Arrange and sew the four units made in step 3, the four corner units made in step 5, and the dark blue D square into rows. Sew the rows together as shown to complete the quilt.

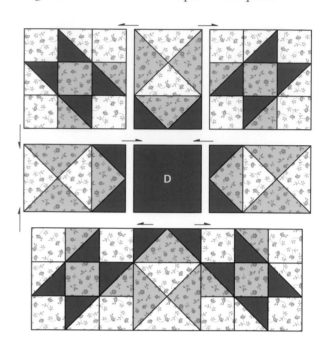

## Finishing

Referring to "Finishing the Quilt" on page 13, piece the backing and then layer the quilt top with the batting and backing. After basting the layers together, quilt or tie as desired. Prepare the binding and sew it to the quilt.

# Pumpkins and Such

*48″ x 48″; by Evelyn Sloppy, 2005*

## Materials

*All yardages are based on 42"-wide fabric.*

8 fat quarters or a total of 2 yards of assorted
gold prints

5 fat quarters or a total of 1¼ yards of assorted
green prints

3¼ yards of fabric for backing

½ yard of fabric for binding

52" x 52" piece of batting

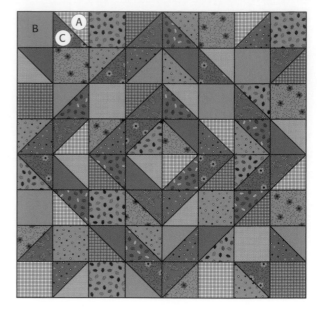

## Cutting

| Fabric | Piece | First Cut | Second Cut |
|---|---|---|---|
| Assorted gold prints | A | 22 squares, 6⅞" x 6⅞" | ◩ |
| | B | 20 squares, 6½" x 6½" | |
| Assorted green prints | C | 22 squares, 6⅞" x 6⅞" | ◩ |
| Binding | | 6 strips, 2½" wide | |

## Piecing

After stitching each unit, press seam allowances as
indicated by arrows in the illustrations.

1.  Using the assorted green and gold triangles, sew
    the green C triangles to the gold A triangles to
    make 44 bias squares.

Make 44.

2.  Arrange and sew the bias squares made in step 1
    and the gold B squares into rows. Sew the rows
    together to complete the quilt.

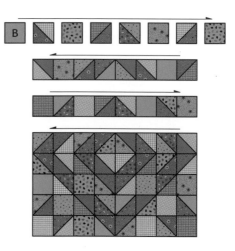

## Finishing

Referring to "Finishing the Quilt" on page 13,
piece the backing and then layer the quilt top with
the batting and backing. After basting the layers
together, quilt or tie as desired. Refer to "Rounded
Corners" on page 17 to shape and bind the edges of
the quilt.

# Schooltime

*15″ x 15″; by Evelyn Sloppy, 2005*

# Materials

*Yardages are based on 42"-wide fabric.*

¾ yard of theme or border print for piecing★

⅝ yard of black print for piecing

⅝ yard of white print for piecing

⅜ yard of yellow print for piecing

3⅛ yards of fabric for backing

½ yard of fabric for binding

49" x 49" piece of batting

★ *If you're using a directional border print, as in the quilt shown, check to see if there are 4 repeats across the width of the fabric. If not, you'll need 1⅓ yards.*

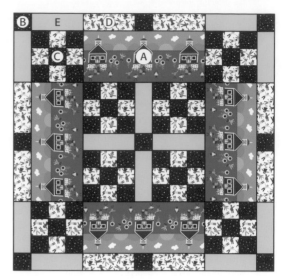

Piece A is a single strip cut from a theme or border print. The photo on page 39 shows yellow strips at the top and bottom of each piece A. These yellow accents are part of the border print, not pieced strips, and have been omitted from the illustrations to avoid confusion.

# Cutting

| Fabric | Piece | Strips | Width | Cut |
|---|---|---|---|---|
| Theme print★ | A | 1 | 21½" | 4 rectangles, 9½" x 21½" |
| Black print | B | 5 | 3½" | 49 squares, 3½" x 3½" |
| White print | C | 3 | 3½" | 32 squares, 3½" x 3½" |
| | D | 2 | 3½" | 8 rectangles, 3½" x 9½" |
| Yellow print | E | 3 | 3½" | 12 rectangles, 3½" x 9½" |
| Binding | | 5 | 2½" | |

★ If you're using a directional print, cut 4 strips, 9½" wide, parallel to the selvage and with the motifs centered. Cut 4 rectangles, 9½" x 21½".

# Piecing

After stitching each unit, press seam allowances as indicated by arrows in the illustrations.

1. Arrange and sew five black B squares and four white C squares into rows. Sew the rows together as shown to make a nine-patch unit. Repeat to make eight units.

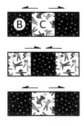

Make 8.

2. Arrange and sew four nine-patch units made in step 1, four yellow E rectangles, and one black B square into rows. Sew the rows together as shown to make the center of the quilt.

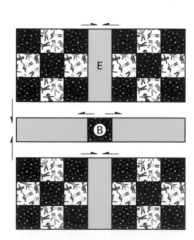

3. Sew theme-print A rectangles to opposite sides of the center unit. Sew a nine-patch unit made in step 1 to each end of the remaining theme-print A rectangles. Sew these units to the top and bottom of the center unit.

5. Sew units made in step 4 to opposite sides of the block. Sew black B squares to the ends of the remaining units made in step 4 as shown. Sew these units to the top and bottom of the center unit to complete the quilt top.

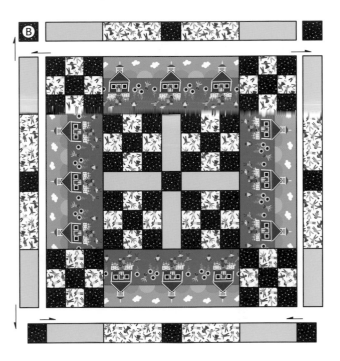

4. Sew one black B square, two white D rectangles, and two yellow E rectangles together as shown for the borders. Repeat to make four units.

Make 4.

# Finishing

Referring to "Finishing the Quilt" on page 13, piece the backing, and then layer the quilt top with the batting and backing. After basting the layers together, quilt or tie as desired. Prepare the binding and sew it to the quilt.

# A Simple Basket

*47¼″ x 47¼″; by Evelyn Sloppy, 2005*

# Materials

*All yardages are based on 42"-wide fabric.*

1¼ yards of light background print for piecing

1⅛ yards of blue print for piecing

1⅛ yards of pink print for piecing (⅝ yard) and
   binding (½ yard)

3¼ yards of fabric for backing

51" x 51" piece of batting

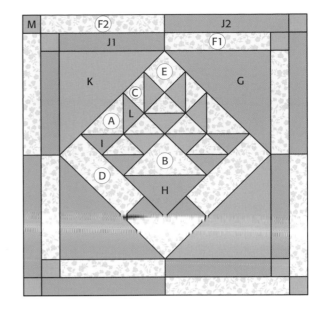

## Cutting

| Fabric | Piece | Strips | Width | First Cut | Second Cut |
|--------|-------|--------|-------|-----------|------------|
| Light background print | A★ | 1 | 11¼" | 1 square, 11¼" x 11¼" | ⊠ |
| | B | From remainder of A strip | | 1 square, 10⅞" x 10⅞" | ◿ |
| | C★ | 1 | 5⅞" | 4 squares, 5⅞" x 5⅞" | ◿ |
| | D | 1 | 5½" | 2 rectangles, 5½" x 15½" | |
| | E | From remainder of D strip | | 1 square, 5½" x 5½" | |
| | F1 and F2 | 4 | 3½" | 4 rectangles, 3½" x 18⅛" (F1) | |
| | | | | 4 rectangles, 3½" x 21⅛" (F2) | |
| Blue print | G | 1 | 18½" | 1 square, 18½" x 18½" | ◿ |
| | H★ | From remainder of G strip | | 1 square, 10⅞" x 10⅞" | ◿ |
| | I | From remainder of G strip | | 3 squares, 5⅞" x 5⅞" | ◿ |
| | J1 and J2 | 4 | 3½" | 4 rectangles, 3½" x 18⅛" (J1) | |
| | | | | 4 rectangles, 3½" x 21⅛" (J2) | |
| Pink print | K | 1 | 18½" | 1 square, 18½" x 18½" | ◿ |
| | L★ | From remainder of K strip | | 4 squares, 5⅞" x 5⅞" | ◿ |
| | M | From remainder of K strip | | 8 squares, 3½" x 3½" | |
| | Binding | 6 | 2½" | | |

★You will have some triangles of these pieces left over after piecing your quilt. Add these to your scrap bag.

# Piecing

After stitching each unit, press seam allowances as indicated by arrows in the illustrations.

1. Sew a background B triangle to a blue H triangle to make a bias square. In the same manner, make five bias squares using a background C triangle and a pink L triangle and two bias squares using a background C triangle and a blue I triangle.

Make 1.  Make 5.  Make 2.

2. Sew together one pink and one blue small bias square made in step 1 as shown. Sew together two pink and one blue bias squares as shown. Sew these to the large bias square made in step 1.

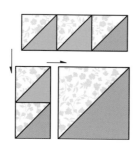

3. Sew a blue I triangle and a pink L triangle to a background A triangle as shown to make a flying-geese unit. Repeat to make two units, making sure the blue is on the left for one unit and on the right for the other unit.

Make 1.  Make 1.

4. Sew a pink bias square to a flying-geese unit as shown. Sew a pink bias square and a background E square to the other flying-geese unit as shown. Pay close attention that you are sewing the pieces together correctly. Sew these units to the center unit made in step 2.

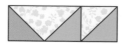 

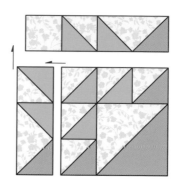

5. Sew a blue I triangle to one end of each background D rectangle as shown. Sew these units to the center unit as shown. Sew a background B triangle to the corner to complete the basket.

Make 1.  Make 1.

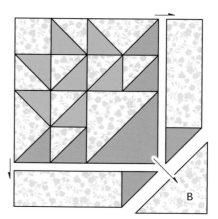

6. Sew pink K triangles to opposite sides of the Basket block. Sew a blue G triangle to the remaining sides. Your block should measure 35¾" square.

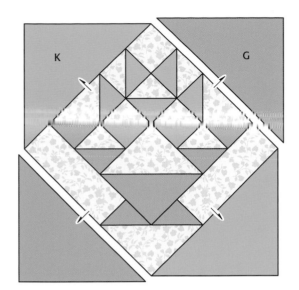

7. To make the inner border, sew a blue J1 piece and a background F1 piece together. Repeat to make four units. Sew units to opposite sides of the Basket block as shown. Sew pink M squares to the ends of the remaining inner-border units. Sew these to the top and bottom of the Basket block.

8. To make the outer border and complete the quilt, repeat step 7 using the blue J2 pieces, the background F2 pieces, and the remaining pink M squares.

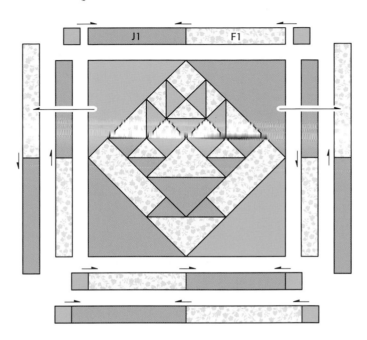

## Finishing

Referring to "Finishing the Quilt" on page 13, piece the backing and then layer the quilt top with the batting and backing. After basting the layers together, quilt or tie as desired. Prepare the binding and sew it to the quilt.

# Springtime

*50″ x 50″; by Evelyn Sloppy, 2005*

# Materials

*All yardages are based on 42"-wide fabric.*

1⅛ yards of light yellow print for piecing

⅞ yard of purple print for piecing (⅜ yard) and
    binding (½ yard)

¾ yard of green print for piecing

⅝ yard of light green print for piecing

½ yard of yellow-and-purple print for piecing

3⅜ yards of fabric for backing

54" x 54" piece of batting

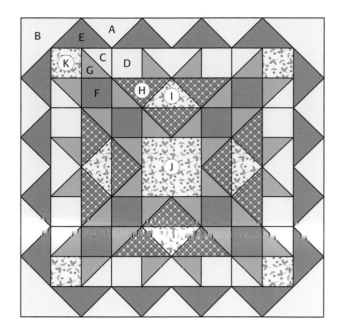

# Cutting

| Fabric | Piece | Strips | Width | First Cut | Second Cut |
|---|---|---|---|---|---|
| Light yellow print | A | 2 | 11¼" | 4 squares, 11¼" x 11¼" | ⊠ |
| | B | From remainder of A strips | | 2 squares, 10⅞" x 10⅞" | ◺ |
| | C | 1 | 5⅞" | 4 squares, 5⅞" x 5⅞" | ◺ |
| | D | From remainder of C strip | | 2 squares, 5½" x 5½" | |
| | D | 1 | 5½" | 6 squares, 5½" x 5½" | |
| Green print | E | 2 | 11¼" | 4 squares, 11¼" x 11¼" | ⊠ |
| | F | From remainder of E strips | | 8 squares, 5½" x 5½" | |
| Light green print | G | 3 | 5⅞" | 16 squares, 5⅞" x 5⅞" | ◺ |
| Purple print | H | 1 | 11¼" | 3 squares, 11¼" x 11¼" | ⊠ |
| | Binding | 6 | 2½" | | |
| Yellow-and-purple print | I | 1 | 11¼" | 1 square, 11¼" x 11¼" | ⊠ |
| | J | From remainder of I strip | | 1 square, 10½" x 10½" | |
| | K | From remainder of I strip | | 4 squares, 5½" x 5½" | |

# Piecing

After stitching each unit, press seam allowances as indicated by arrows in the illustrations.

1. Sew light green G triangles to the short sides of a purple H triangle as shown to make a flying-geese unit. Repeat to make four units. In the same manner, make four flying-geese units using two light green G triangles and a light yellow A triangle for each unit.

Make 4.　　Make 4.

2. Arrange and sew four purple flying-geese units made in step 1, four green F squares, and the yellow-and-purple J square into rows as shown. Sew the rows together to complete the center star.

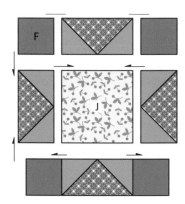

3. Sew purple H triangles to the short sides of a yellow-and-purple I triangle as shown. Sew a light green G triangle to each end of the unit. Repeat to make four units.

Make 4.

Make 4.

4. Sew units from step 3 to opposite sides of the center star unit. Sew green F squares to each end of the remaining units. Sew these units to the top and bottom of the center star unit.

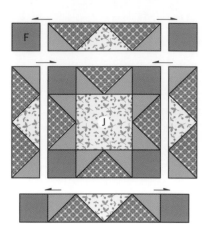

5. Sew a light green G triangle to a light yellow C triangle to make a bias square. Repeat to make eight units.

Make 8.

6. Sew together two of the bias squares made in step 5, two light yellow D squares, and a light yellow flying-geese unit made in step 1 as shown. Repeat to make four units. Sew one unit to each side of the center block.

Make 4.

7. Sew a yellow-and-purple K square to each end of the remaining units. Sew these units to the top and bottom of the center unit.

8. Sew together four green E triangles and three light yellow A triangles as shown. Repeat to make four units.

Make 4.

9. Sew a unit made in step 7 to each side of the center unit. Sew a light yellow B triangle to each corner to complete the quilt top.

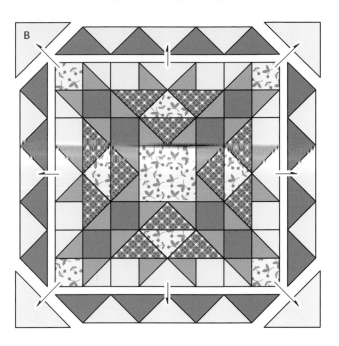

## Finishing

Referring to "Finishing the Quilt" on page 13, piece the backing and then layer the quilt top with the batting and backing. After basting the layers together, quilt or tie as desired. Prepare the binding and sew it to the quilt.

## Try It a Different Way

Change the look of the quilt by switching the placement of your lights and darks.

# Star Bright

*48" x 48"; by Evelyn Sloppy, 2005*

# Materials

*All yardages are based on 42"-wide fabric.*

1⅛ yards of purple print for piecing

1 yard of pink print for piecing (⅝ yard) and
   binding (½ yard)

⅝ yard of green print for piecing

⅝ yard of light print 1 for piecing★

½ yard of light print 2 for piecing★

3¼ yards of fabric for backing

52" x 52" piece of batting

★*1 yard will be sufficient if you choose to use only
one light print.*

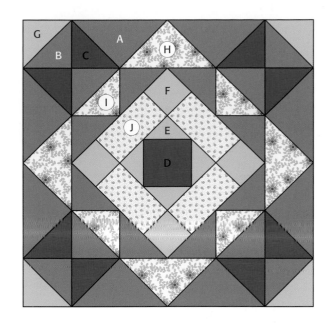

# Cutting

| Fabric | Piece | Strips | Width | First Cut | Second Cut |
|--------|-------|--------|-------|-----------|------------|
| Purple print | A | 1 | 17¼" | 2 squares, 17¼" x 17¼" | ⊠ |
| | B | 2 | 8⅞" | 8 squares, 8⅞" x 8⅞" | ◺ |
| Pink print | C | 1 | 8⅞" | 4 squares, 8⅞" x 8⅞" | ◺ |
| | D | 1 | 8½" | 1 square, 8½" x 8½" | |
| | Binding | 6 | 2½" | | |
| Green print | E | 1 | 6½" | 2 squares, 6½" x 6½" | ◺ |
| | F | From remainder of E strip | | 4 squares, 6⅛" x 6⅛" | |
| | G | 1 | 8⅞" | 2 squares, 8⅞" x 8⅞" | ◺ |
| Light print 1 | H | 1 | 17¼" | 1 square, 17¼" x 17¼" | ⊠ |
| | I | From remainder of H strip | | 2 squares, 8⅞" x 8⅞" | ◺ |
| Light print 2 | J | 1 | 11¾" | 4 rectangles, 6⅛" x 11¾" | |

# Piecing

After stitching each unit, press seam allowances as
indicated by arrows in the illustrations.

1. Sew a green E triangle to each side of the pink
   D square.

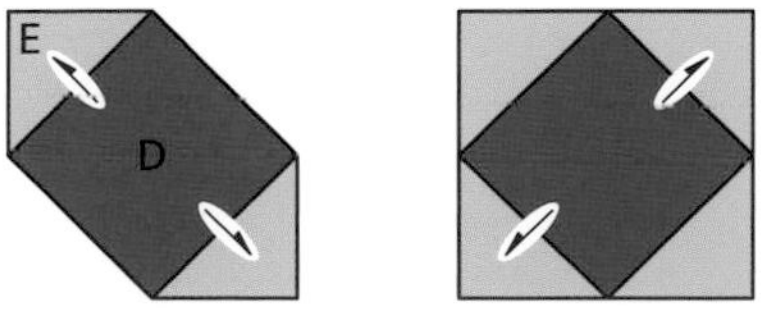

2. Sew light print J rectangles to opposite sides of
   the unit made in step 1. Sew green F squares to
   each end of a light
   print J rectangle.
   Repeat to make
   two units. Sew
   these units to the
   remaining sides
   to make the cen-
   ter unit.

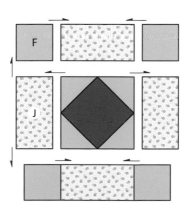

3. Sew a purple B triangle to a light print I triangle to make a bias square. Repeat to make four units. In the same manner, make four bias squares using a purple B triangle and a green G triangle.

Make 4.        Make 4.

4. Sew a purple B triangle to adjacent sides of a bias square made in step 3. Repeat to make four units. Sew these to the sides of the center unit made in step 2.

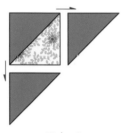

Make 4.

5. Sew together two purple A triangles, one light print H triangle, and two pink C triangles as shown to make the border unit. Repeat to make four units.

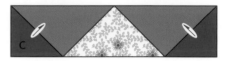

Make 4.

6. Sew border units to opposite sides of the center unit. Sew the remaining bias squares made in step 3 to each end of the remaining border units. Sew these to the top and bottom to complete the quilt top.

# Finishing

Referring to "Finishing the Quilt" on page 13, piece the backing and then layer the quilt top with the batting and backing. After basting the layers together, quilt or tie as desired. Refer to "Rounded Corners" on page 17 to shape and bind the edges of the quilt.

# Star within a Star

*50″ x 50″; by Evelyn Sloppy, 2005*

# Materials

*All yardages are based on 42"-wide fabric.*

7 fat quarters of assorted tan prints or 1⅝ yards total
  of a single print or assorted tan prints for piecing

6 fat quarters of assorted blue prints or 1⅜ yards total
  of a single print or assorted blue prints for piecing

4 fat quarters of assorted red prints or ⅝ yard total
  of a single print or assorted red prints for piecing

3⅜ yards of fabric for backing

½ yard of fabric for binding

54" x 54" piece of batting

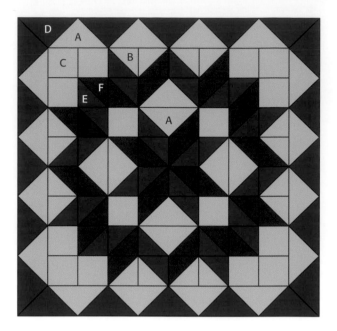

# Cutting

| Fabric | Piece | First Cut | Second Cut |
|---|---|---|---|
| Tan prints | A | 6 squares, 11¼" x 11¼" | ⊠ |
| | B | 8 squares, 5⅞" x 5⅞" | ◺ |
| | C | 16 squares, 5½" x 5½" | |
| Blue prints | D | 5 squares, 11¼" x 11¼" | ⊠ |
| | E | 16 squares, 5⅞" x 5⅞" | ◺ |
| Red prints | F | 16 squares, 5⅞" x 5⅞" | ◺ |
| Binding | | 6 strips, 2½" wide | |

# Piecing

If you want to use the same fabric for both triangles of each star point, as in the project shown, lay out all the pieces first, matching as you go, before you start sewing. You can avoid this step by sewing the triangles together randomly.

1. Sew a blue E triangle to a red F triangle to make a bias square. Repeat to make 16 units. In the same manner, make eight bias squares using a tan B triangle and a blue E triangle and eight bias squares using a tan B triangle and a red F triangle.

Make 16.

Make 8.

Make 8.

2. Sew a red F triangle and a blue E triangle to a tan A triangle as shown to make a flying-geese unit. Take care that the triangles are positioned correctly. Repeat to make eight units.

Make 8.

3. Sew together four blue-and-red bias squares as shown. Sew two flying-geese units to the sides of the center pinwheel unit. Sew a tan C square to both ends of two flying-geese units. Sew these to the top and bottom of the pinwheel unit to make the center star.

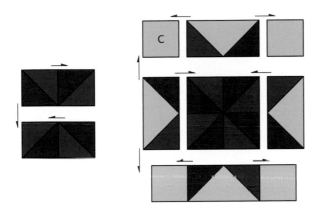

4. Sew two blue-and-tan bias squares to two red-and-tan bias squares, alternating them as shown. Repeat to make four units. Sew a blue-and-red bias square to each end of a flying-geese unit. Repeat to make four units. Sew one of each unit together. Repeat to make four units.

Make 4. Make 4.

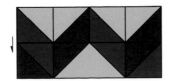

Make 4.

5. Sew two assorted tan C squares together. Repeat to make four units. Sew a tan C square to a blue-and-red bias square. Repeat to make four units. Sew one of each unit together. Repeat to make four units.

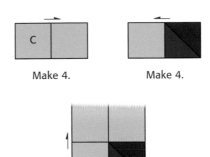

Make 4. Make 4.

Make 4.

6. Sew units made in step 4 to opposite sides of the center star.

7. Sew a unit made in step 5 to each end of the remaining units from step 4. Sew these sections to the remaining sides of the center star.

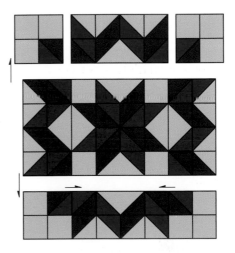

8. Sew together four tan A triangles and three blue D triangles as shown. Repeat to make four border units.

Make 4.

9. Sew two blue D triangles together along their short sides. Repeat to make four units.

Make 4.

10. Sew border units made in step 8 to each side of the center section. Then sew the triangle units made in step 9 to the corners to complete the quilt top.

## Finishing

Referring to "Finishing the Quilt" on page 13, piece the backing and then layer the quilt top with the batting and backing. After basting the layers together, quilt or tie as desired. Prepare the binding and sew it to the quilt.

## Try It a Different Way

Instead of gathering assorted prints in three muted colors, try this design using just three bright prints.

# Stars and Stripes

*56" x 56"; by Evelyn Sloppy, 2005*

# Materials

*All yardages are based on 42″-wide fabric.*

1⅝ yards of pink print for piecing (1⅛ yards)
    and binding (½ yard)

1½ yards of light print for piecing

1⅛ yards of striped print for piecing

¾ yard of brown print for piecing

3⅝ yards of fabric for backing

60" x 60" piece of batting

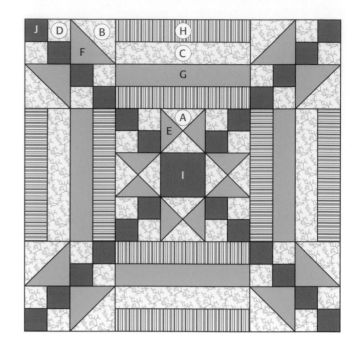

# Cutting

| Fabric | Piece | Strips | Width | First Cut | Second Cut |
|---|---|---|---|---|---|
| Light print | A | 1 | 9¼" | 2 squares, 9¼" x 9¼" | ⊠ |
| | B | 1 | 8⅞" | 4 squares, 8⅞" x 8⅞" | ◹ |
| | C | 6 | 4½" | 4 rectangles, 4½" x 24½" | |
| | D | From remainder of C strip | | 24 squares, 4½" x 4½" | |
| Pink print | E | 1 | 9¼" | 2 squares, 9¼" x 9¼" | ⊠ |
| | F | 1 | 8⅞" | 4 squares, 8⅞" x 8⅞" | ◹ |
| | G | 4 | 4½" | 4 rectangles, 4½" x 24½" | |
| | Binding | 6 | 2½" | | |
| Striped print | H | 8 | 4½" | 8 rectangles, 4½" x 24½" | |
| Brown print | I | 1 | 8½" | 1 square, 8½" x 8½" | |
| | J | 3 | 4½" | 24 squares, 4½" x 4½" | |

# Piecing

After stitching each unit, press seam allowances as indicated by arrows in the illustrations.

1. Sew light A and pink E triangles in pairs as shown. Sew the pairs together to make four quarter-square-triangle units.

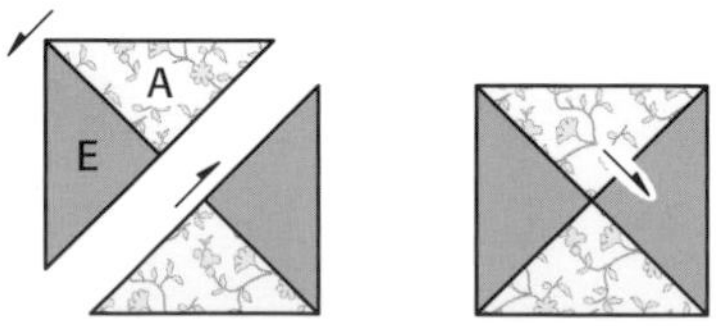

Make 4.

2. Sew a light B triangle to a pink F triangle to make a bias square. Repeat to make eight units.

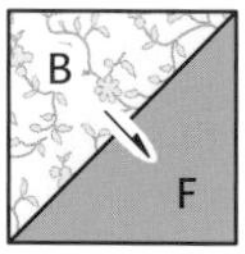

Make 8.

3. Sew together two light D squares and two brown J squares as shown to make a four-patch unit. Repeat to make 12 units.

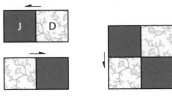

Make 12.

4. Arrange and sew the four units from step 1, four of the units from step 3, and the brown I square into rows. Sew the rows together to make the center star unit.

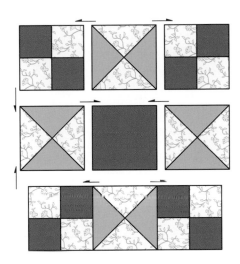

5. Sew together two of the bias squares from step 2 and two of the units from step 3 to make the corner unit. Repeat to make four units.

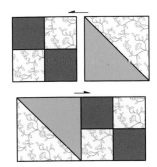 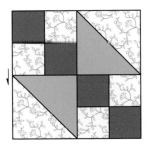

Make 4.

6. Sew together two striped H rectangles, one light C rectangle, and one pink G rectangle as shown to make a side unit. Repeat to make four units.

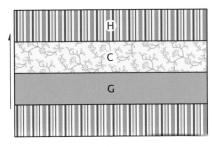

Make 4.

7. Arrange and sew the four corner units, the four units made in step 6, and the center star into rows. Sew the rows together to complete the quilt top.

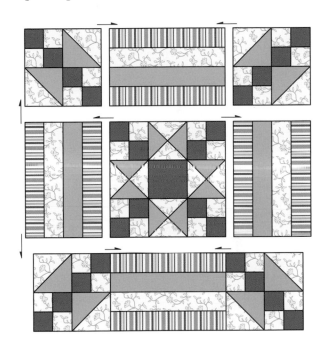

# Finishing

Referring to "Finishing the Quilt" on page 13, piece the backing and then layer the quilt top with the batting and backing. After basting the layers together, quilt or tie as desired. Prepare the binding and sew it to the quilt.

# Starburst

*48" x 48"; by Evelyn Sloppy, 2005*

# Materials

*All yardages are based on 42″-wide fabric.*

1⅛ yards of light tan print for piecing

1⅛ yards of medium tan print for piecing

1⅛ yards of red print for piecing (¾ yard) and
 binding (½ yard)

⅝ yard of navy blue print for piecing

3¼ yards of fabric for backing

52″ x 52″ piece of batting

# Cutting

| Fabric | Piece | Strips | Width | First Cut | Second Cut |
|---|---|---|---|---|---|
| Light tan print | A | 1 | 13¼" | 3 squares, 13¼" x 13¼" | ⊠ |
| | B | 1 | 7¼" | 2 squares, 7¼" x 7¼" | ⊠ |
| | C | From remainder of B strip | | 1 square, 6⅞" x 6⅞" | ◹ |
| | C | 1 | 6⅞" | 5 squares, 6⅞" x 6⅞" | ◹ |
| | D | 1 | 6½" | 4 squares, 6½" x 6½" | |
| Medium tan print | E | 1 | 13¼" | 2 squares, 13¼" x 13¼" | ⊠ |
| | F | 2 | 6⅞" | 10 squares, 6⅞" x 6⅞" | ◹ |
| | G | 1 | 9¾" | 2 squares, 9¾" x 9¾" | ⊠ |
| Red print | H | 1 | 7¼" | 2 squares, 7¼" x 7¼" | ⊠ |
| | I | 1 | 6⅞" | 4 squares, 6⅞" x 6⅞" | ◹ |
| | J | 1 | 6½" | 4 squares, 6½" x 6½" | |
| | Binding | 6 | 2½" | | |
| Navy blue print | K | 1 | 9¾" | 2 squares, 9¾" x 9¾" | ⊠ |
| | L | 1 | 6⅞" | 4 squares, 6⅞"x 6⅞" | ◹ |

# Piecing

With so many triangle points meeting on this quilt, I like to press all the seams open for less bulk. Give it a try; you might also prefer this method. However, traditional pressing arrows and instructions are shown for each step.

1. Sew medium tan G triangles and navy blue K triangles together in pairs as shown. Make eight of these units. Sew the units together in pairs to make four quarter-square-triangle units.

Make 4.

2. Sew the four units from step 1 together as shown to make the center pinwheel unit. Be careful to arrange the units as shown.

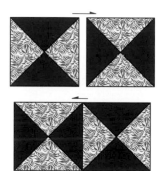

3. Sew the light tan B triangles and red H triangles together in pairs. Make four units with the red triangles on the right and four with the red triangles on the left as shown. Join these units to adjacent sides of the red J squares as shown. Pay careful attention to the color placement. Make four.

Make 4.    Make 4.

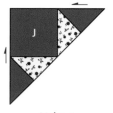

Make 4.

4. Sew two of the units made in step 3 to opposite sides of the center pinwheel unit. Sew the remaining two units to the other sides of the center pinwheel unit.

5. Sew a light tan C triangle to a medium tan F triangle to make a bias square. Repeat to make 12 units. In the same manner, sew red I triangles to medium tan F triangles to make eight units.

Make 12.    Make 8.

6. Sew together two red and two tan bias squares from step 5 as shown. Repeat to make four units.

Make 4.

7. Sew two of the units made in step 6 to opposite sides of the center unit. Sew the remaining tan bias squares made in step 5 to each end of the

remaining units made in step 6 as shown. Sew these to the top and bottom of the center unit.

8. Sew three light tan A triangles and two medium tan E triangles together as shown. Sew a navy blue L triangle to each end. Repeat to make four units.

Make 4.

9. Sew two of the units made in step 8 to opposite sides of the center unit. Sew a light tan D square to each end of the remaining units made in step 8. Sew these units to the top and bottom of the center unit to complete the quilt top.

## Finishing

Referring to "Finishing the Quilt" on page 13, piece the backing and then layer the quilt top with the batting and backing. After basting the layers together, quilt or tie as desired. Refer to "Rounded Corners" on page 17 to shape and bind the edges of the quilt.

# Strawberries 'n' Cream

*48" x 48"; by Evelyn Sloppy, 2005*

# Materials

*All yardages are based on 42″-wide fabric.*

1⅛ yards of green print for piecing

1 yard of red print for piecing (½ yard) and
   binding (½ yard)

⅞ yard of light yellow print for piecing

⅝ yard of medium yellow print for piecing

3¼ yards of fabric for backing

52" x 52" piece of batting

# Cutting

| Fabric | Piece | Strips | Width | First Cut | Second Cut |
|---|---|---|---|---|---|
| Green print | A | 1 | 13¼" | 1 square, 13¼" x 13¼" | ⊠ |
| | B | 1 | 9" | 4 squares, 9" x 9" | |
| | C | 2 | 6⅞" | 8 squares, 6⅞" x 6⅞" | � |
| | D | From remainder of C strip | | 4 squares, 6½" x 6½" | |
| Medium yellow print | E | 1 | 12½" | 1 square, 12½" x 12½" | |
| | F | From remainder of E strip | | 3 squares, 6⅞" x 6⅞" | ◩ |
| | F | 1 | 6⅞" | 5 squares, 6⅞" x 6⅞" | ◩ |
| Light yellow print | G | 1 | 13¼" | 2 squares, 13¼" x 13¼" | ⊠ |
| | H | 2 | 6⅞" | 8 squares, 6⅞" x 6⅞" | ◩ |
| | I | From remainder of G and H strips | | 4 squares, 6½" x 6½" | |
| Red print | J | 1 | 6⅞" | 4 squares, 6⅞" x 6⅞" | ◩ |
| | K | 1 | 6½" | 4 squares, 6½" x 6½" | |
| | Binding | 6 | 2½" | | |

# Piecing

After stitching each unit, press seam allowances as indicated by arrows in the illustrations.

1. Sew a medium yellow F triangle to a light yellow H triangle to make a bias square. Repeat to make eight units. In the same manner, make eight bias squares using green C triangles and the remaining light yellow H triangles.

Make 8.           Make 8.

2. Sew two red J triangles and two medium yellow F triangles to a green B square as shown. Repeat to make four units.

Make 4.

3. Sew together two of the yellow bias squares, a green D square, and a red K square as shown. Repeat to make four units.

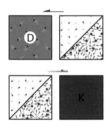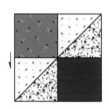

Make 4.

4. Arrange and sew the four units made in step 2, the four units made in step 3, and the medium yellow E square into rows. Sew the rows together to make the center star.

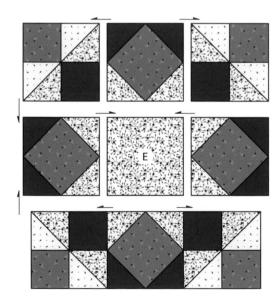

5. Sew together two light yellow G triangles, one green A triangle, and two green C triangles as shown. Sew a green bias square to each end. Repeat to make four border units.

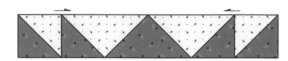

Make 4.

6. Sew border units to opposite sides of the center star. Sew a light yellow I square to each end of the remaining border units. Sew these units to the top and bottom of the center star to complete the quilt top.

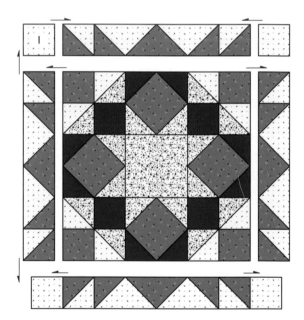

# Finishing

Referring to "Finishing the Quilt" on page 13, piece the backing and then layer the quilt top with the batting and backing. After basting the layers together, quilt or tie as desired. Refer to "Rounded Corners" on page 17 to shape and bind the edges of the quilt.

# Triple Bear's Paw

*54" x 54"; by Evelyn Sloppy, 2005*

# Materials

*All yardages are based on 42"-wide fabric.*

2⅜ yards of blue print for piecing (2 yards) and
  binding (½ yard)

1½ yards of cream print for piecing

3⅝ yards of fabric for backing

58" x 58" piece of batting

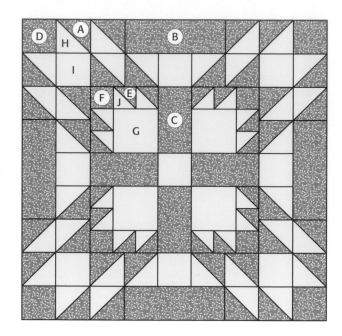

# Cutting

| Fabric | Piece | Strips | Width | First Cut | Second Cut |
|--------|-------|--------|-------|-----------|------------|
| Blue print | A | 4 | 6⅞" | 16 squares, 6⅞" x 6⅞" | ◩ |
| | B | 2 | 6½" | 4 rectangles, 6½" x 18½" | |
| | C | 2 | 6½" | 4 rectangles, 6½" x 12½" | |
| | D | From remainder of C strips | | 4 squares, 6½" x 6½" | |
| | E | 1 | 4⅞" | 8 squares, 4⅞" x 4⅞" | ◩ |
| | F | 1 | 4½" | 4 squares, 4½" x 4½" | |
| | Binding | 6 | 2½" | | |
| Cream print | G | 1 | 8½" | 4 squares, 8½" x 8½" | |
| | H | 4 | 6⅞" | 16 squares, 6⅞" x 6⅞" | ◩ |
| | I | From remainder of H strips | | 3 squares, 6½" x 6½" | |
| | I | 1 | 6½" | 6 squares, 6½" x 6½" | |
| | J | 1 | 4⅞" | 8 squares, 4⅞" x 4⅞" | ◩ |

## Cutting the Bias Squares

Place the 6⅞" blue and cream strips right sides together
before you cut the squares. Then, after making the initial
cuts for the squares, cut the squares once diagonally and
the pieces will be ready to sew together to make the bias
squares. Do the same with the 4⅞" blue and cream strips.

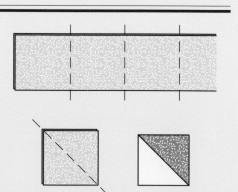

# Piecing

After stitching each unit, press seam allowances as indicated by arrows in the illustrations.

1. Sew a blue A triangle to a cream H triangle to make a bias square. Repeat to make 32 units. In the same manner, make 16 bias squares using the blue E triangles and the cream J triangles.

Make 32.         Make 16.

2. Sew together the smaller bias squares from step 1. You need four pairs facing one direction and four pairs facing in the opposite direction as shown. Join the bias squares, a blue F square, and a cream G square as shown. Repeat to make four of these units.

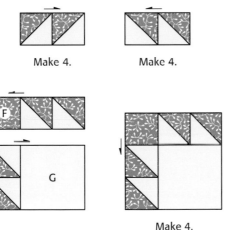

Make 4.         Make 4.

Make 4.

3. Arrange and sew the four units made in step 2, four blue C rectangles, and one cream I square

into rows. Sew the rows together to make the center bear's paw unit.

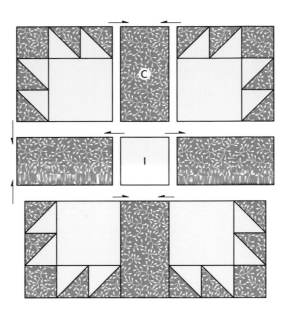

4. Sew a large bias square made in step 1 to each end of a blue B rectangle as shown. Sew two large bias squares made in step 1 to opposite sides of one cream I square, paying careful attention to the color placement. Repeat to make four units.

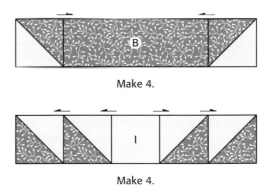

Make 4.

Make 4.

5. Join one of each unit from step 4 to make four border units.

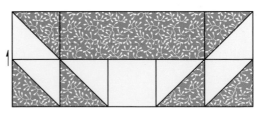

Make 4.

6. Sew together two large bias squares made in step 1, one blue D square, and one cream I square as shown to make a corner unit. Repeat to make four units.

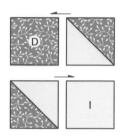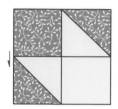

Make 4.

7. Arrange and sew the center bear's paw unit, the border units made in step 5, and the corner units made in step 6 into rows. Sew the rows together to complete the quilt top.

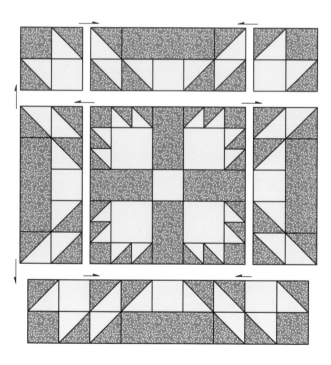

## Finishing

Referring to "Finishing the Quilt" on page 13, piece the backing and then layer the quilt top with the batting and backing. After basting the layers together, quilt or tie as desired. Refer to "Rounded Corners" on page 17 to shape and bind the edges of the quilt.

### Try It a Different Way

Make a scrappy bear's paw unit by using up leftover light and dark fabrics from your stash.

# Vintage Star

*48″ x 48″; by Evelyn Sloppy, 2005*

# Materials

*All yardages are based on 42"-wide fabric.*

1⅛ yards of brown print for piecing

1⅛ yards of light tan print for piecing

1 yard of rust print for piecing (½ yard) and
    binding (½ yard)

⅔ yard of medium tan print for piecing

3¼ yards of fabric for backing

52" x 52" piece of batting

# Cutting

| Fabric | Piece | Strips | Width | First Cut | Second Cut |
|---|---|---|---|---|---|
| Brown print | A | 1 | 7¼" | 2 squares, 7¼" x 7¼" | ⊠ |
| | B | 1 | 6⅞" | 4 squares, 6⅞" x 6⅞" | ◺ |
| | C | 3 | 6½" | 16 squares, 6½" x 6½" | |
| Light tan print | D | 1 | 13¼" | 1 square, 13¼" x 13¼" | ⊠ |
| | E | 1 | 6⅞" | 4 squares, 6⅞" x 6⅞" | ◺ |
| | F | 2 | 6½" | 12 squares, 6½" x 6½" | |
| Medium tan print | G | 1 | 13¼" | 1 square, 13¼" x 13¼" | ⊠ |
| | H | From remainder of G strip | | 1 square, 12½" x 12½" | |
| | I | From remainder of G strip | | 4 squares, 4¾" x 4¾" | |
| | J | 1 | 6⅞" | 4 squares, 6⅞" x 6⅞" | ◺ |
| Rust print | K | 2 | 6⅞" | 8 squares, 6⅞" x 6⅞" | ◺ |
| | Binding | 6 | 2½" | | |

# Piecing

After stitching each unit, press seam allowances as indicated by arrows in the illustrations.

1.  Sew brown A triangles to two adjacent sides of a medium tan I square. Sew rust K triangles to the two short sides of these units. Repeat to make four units.

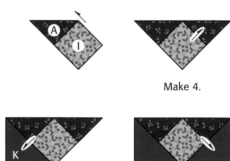

Make 4.

Make 4.

2. Sew a rust K triangle to a light tan E triangle to make a bias square. Repeat to make eight units.

Make 8.

3. Sew brown B triangles to the short sides of a medium tan G triangle to make a flying-geese unit. Repeat to make four units. In the same manner, make four flying-geese units using two medium tan J triangles and a light tan D triangle for each unit.

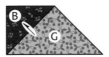

Make 4.

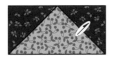

Make 4.

4. Arrange and sew four brown C squares, three light tan F squares, and two of the bias squares made in step 2 into rows. Sew the rows together to make a corner unit. Repeat to make four units.

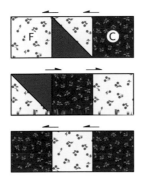

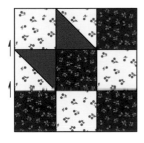

Make 4.

5. Sew together one light and one dark flying-geese unit with one unit made in step 1 as shown. Repeat to make four units.

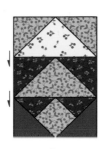

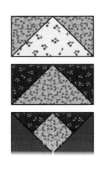

Make 4.

6. Arrange and sew the corner units, the four units made in step 5, and the medium tan H square into rows. Sew the rows together to complete the quilt top.

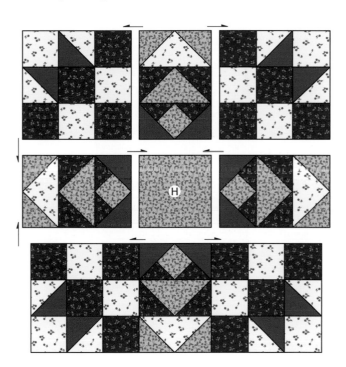

# Finishing

Referring to "Finishing the Quilt" on page 13, piece the backing and then layer the quilt top with the batting and backing. After basting the layers together, quilt or tie as desired. Prepare the binding and sew it to the quilt.

# Wild Goose Chase

*45" x 45"; by Evelyn Sloppy, 2005*

# Materials

*All yardages are based on 42"-wide fabric.*

1⅜ yards of black print for piecing (1 yard) and
   binding (½ yard)

⅞ yard of tan print for piecing

⅞ yard of medium green print for piecing

⅜ yard of light green print for piecing

3⅛ yards of fabric for backing

49" x 49" piece of batting

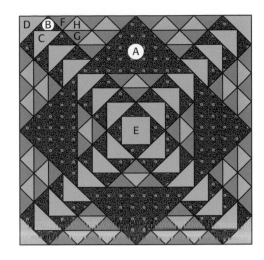

# Cutting

| Fabric | Piece | Strips | Width | First Cut | Second Cut |
|--------|-------|--------|-------|-----------|------------|
| Black print | A | 1 | 16¾" | 2 squares, 16⅞" x 16⅞" | ◻ |
| | B | 3 | 4⅞" | 22 squares, 4⅞" x 4⅞" | ◻ |
| | Binding | 5 | 2½" | | |
| Tan print | C | 2 | 9¼" | 5 squares, 9¼" x 9¼" | ⊠ |
| | D | 1 | 6½" | 4 squares, 6½" x 6½" | ◻ |
| | E | From remainder of D strip | | 1 square, 6⅛" x 6⅛" | |
| Medium green print | F | 2 | 6⅞" | 8 squares, 6⅞" x 6⅞" | ⊠ |
| | G | 2 | 4⅞" | 14 squares, 4⅞" x 4⅞"★ | ◻ |
| Light green print | H | 2 | 4⅞" | 14 squares, 4⅞" x 4⅞"★ | ◻ |

★ Place the 4⅞" strips of medium and light green prints right sides together when you cut the G and H squares. Then, cut the squares once diagonally and the pieces will be ready to sew together to make bias squares.

# Piecing

After stitching each unit, press seam allowances as indicated by arrows in the illustrations.

1. Sew the medium green G triangles to light green H triangles to make 28 bias squares.

Make 28.

2. Sew two black B triangles to the short sides of a tan C triangle to make a flying-geese unit. Repeat to make 20 units.

Make 20.

3. Sew a black B triangle to each side of a tan E square.

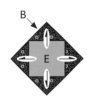

4. Sew two flying-geese units and a tan D triangle together as shown. Repeat to make four units. In the same manner, make four units using three flying-geese units and a tan D triangle.

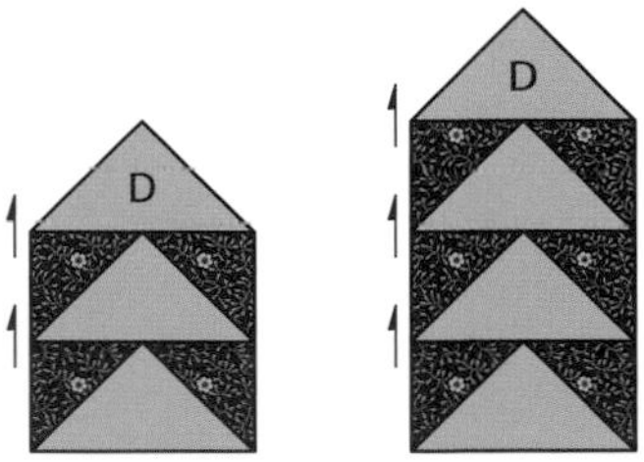

Make 4.          Make 4.

5. Sew together one bias square and two medium green F triangles as shown. Repeat to make four units. In the same manner, make eight units using three bias squares and three medium green F triangles.

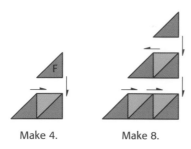

Make 4.  Make 8.

6. Arrange and sew the unit made in step 3, the four small flying-geese units, and the four small units made in step 5 into rows. Sew the rows together to make the center unit.

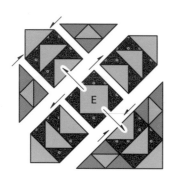

7. Sew a black A triangle to each side of the center unit.

8. Sew together a large flying-geese unit and two large units made in step 5 as shown. Repeat to make four units.

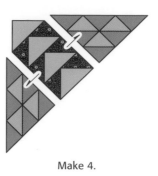

Make 4.

9. Sew the units made in step 8 to each side of the center unit to complete the quilt top.

## Finishing

Referring to "Finishing the Quilt" on page 13, piece the backing and then layer the quilt top with the batting and backing. After basting the layers together, quilt or tie as desired. Prepare the binding and sew it to the quilt.

# Winter Dreams

*50″ x 50″; by Evelyn Sloppy, 2005*

# Materials

*All yardages are based on 42"-wide fabric.*

1 yard of tan-and-red print for piecing

1 yard of light tan print for piecing

⅞ yard of green print for piecing (⅜ yard) and
   binding (½ yard)

¾ yard of olive green print for piecing

⅝ yard of red print for piecing

3⅜ yards of fabric for backing

54" x 54" piece of batting

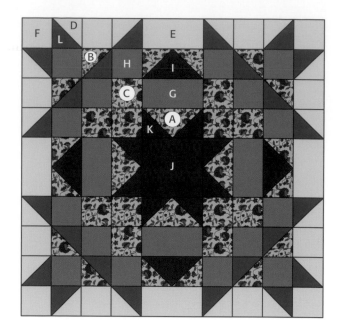

# Cutting

| Fabric | Piece | Strips | Width | First Cut | Second Cut |
|--------|-------|--------|-------|-----------|------------|
| Tan-and-red print | A | 1 | 11¼" | 1 square, 11¼" x 11¼" | ⊠ |
| | B | From remainder of A strip | | 2 squares, 5⅞" x 5⅞" | ◺ |
| | B | 1 | 5⅞" | 6 squares, 5⅞" x 5⅞" | ◺ |
| | C | 2 | 5½" | 12 squares, 5½" x 5½" | |
| Light tan print | D | 2 | 5⅞" | 8 squares, 5⅞" x 5⅞" | ◺ |
| | E | 3 | 5½" | 4 rectangles, 5½" x 10½" | |
| | F | From remainder of E strips | | 12 squares, 5½" x 5½" | |
| Olive green print | G | 4 | 5½" | 4 rectangles, 5½" x 10½" | |
| | H | From remainder of G strips | | 16 squares, 5½" x 5½" | |
| Red print | I | 1 | 11¼" | 1 square, 11¼" x 11¼" | ⊠ |
| | J | From remainder of I strip | | 1 square, 10½" x 10½" | |
| | K | 1 | 5⅞" | 4 squares, 5⅞" x 5⅞" | ◺ |
| Green print | L | 2 | 5⅞" | 12 squares, 5⅞" x 5⅞" | ◺ |
| | Binding | 6 | 2½" | | |

# Piecing

After stitching each unit, press seam allowances as indicated by arrows in the illustrations.

1.  Sew red K triangles to the short sides of a tan-and-red A triangle to make a flying-geese unit. Repeat to make four units. In the same manner, make four flying-geese units using two tan-and-red B triangles and one red I triangle for each unit.

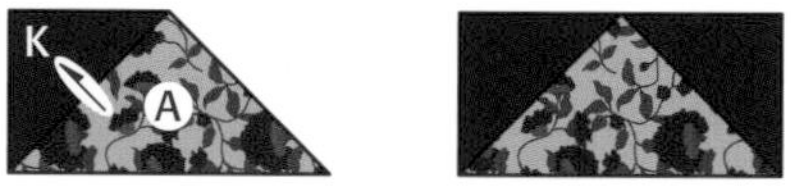

Make 4.

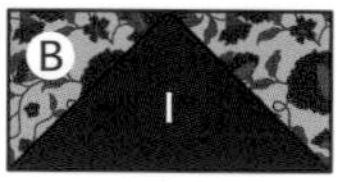

Make 4.

2. Sew the light tan D triangles to the green L triangles to make 16 bias squares. In the same manner, make eight bias squares using tan-and-red B triangles and green L triangles.

Make 16.          Make 8.

3. Arrange and sew three tan-and-red C squares, four olive green H squares, three light tan F squares, and six of the bias squares into rows. Sew the rows together to make a corner unit. Repeat to make four units.

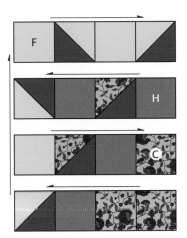

Make 4.

4. Sew together one light tan E rectangle, one olive green G rectangle, and two of the flying-geese units as shown. Repeat to make four units.

Make 4.

5. Arrange and sew the corner units, the four units made in step 4, and the red J square into rows. Sew the rows together to complete the quilt.

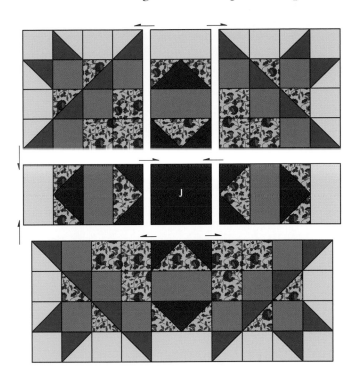

## Finishing

Referring to "Finishing the Quilt" on page 13, piece the backing and then layer the quilt top with the batting and backing. After basting the layers together, quilt or tie as desired. Prepare the binding and sew it to the quilt.

# ABOUT THE AUTHOR

**Evelyn Sloppy** lives with her husband, Dean, on 80 wooded acres in western Washington State, where they enjoy country living. They love to travel and hike, and they look forward to visits from their four children and six grandchildren.

Evelyn has been quilting since 1991. Her favorites are scrappy, traditional quilts, but she also enjoys trying new ideas and stretching her imagination. She loves using new techniques that make quiltmaking faster, more accurate, and just more fun. Although she appreciates hand quilting, she finishes most of her quilts on her long-arm quilting machine. She has made close to 300 quilts, many of them charity quilts. She says that there is no better way for her to give back to her community than by doing what she loves to do—quilting.

This is Evelyn's fifth book with Martingale & Company.